The Fine Print of Christianity

The Fine Print of Christianity

NATHAN SHANE MILLER

WIPF & STOCK · Eugene, Oregon

THE FINE PRINT OF CHRISTIANITY

Copyright © 2011 Nathan Shane Miller. All rights reserved. Except for brief quotations in critical publications or reviews, no part of this book may be reproduced in any manner without prior written permission from the publisher. Write: Permissions, Wipf and Stock Publishers, 199 W. 8th Ave., Suite 3, Eugene, OR 97401.

Wipf & Stock
An Imprint of Wipf and Stock Publishers
199 W. 8th Ave., Suite 3
Eugene, OR 97401
www.wipfandstock.com

ISBN 13: 978-1-60899-707-7

Manufactured in the U.S.A.

Scriptures taken from the Holy Bible, New International Version®, NIV®. Copyright © 1973, 1978, 1984 by Biblica, Inc.™ Used by permission of Zondervan. All rights reserved worldwide. www.zondervan.com.

*To my wife, friend, and patient editor, Ashley,
and to my parents and siblings for their support and gracious praise.*

Contents

Preface ix

1. Jesus Loves You: But He'll Cast You To Hell 1
2. God Is Just: But Life's Not Fair 12
3. God Is The Great Physician: But Sickness and Suffering Persist 24
4. God Has A Plan: But You May Not Like It 35
5. Faith Is A Virtue: But Not All Faith 46
6. Be Joyful Always: But You Won't Feel Like It 57
7. God Provides All Our Needs: But Some Are Homeless And Starving 68
8. Miracles Abound: But Have You Ever Seen One? 79
9. Prayer Is Effective: But When You Keep Praying Does Anything Happen? 88
10. In Everything Glorify God: But Life Seems Indifferent To Glory 99

Conclusion 111
Bibliography 113

Preface

Caveat emptor, let the buyer beware, is the adage of a free and unregulated market. It is a word of caution, an exhortation to scrutinize, and a reminder that not everything is as it appears. As consumers we have learned, sometimes the hard way, that big flashy deals have small print terms and conditions, and we have grown to expect the caveats and catches concealed in the sales pitch. And just as the commercial market is full of lofty promises and glossed over particulars, so it is with the marketplace of ideas. In the same way it behooves us to read the fine print of our acquisitions, it would befit us to study the fine print of our own beliefs, even our most cherished ones. Even Christianity.

There might be some who balk at the idea of fine print in Christianity. They might argue that fine print is a legal safety net for otherwise misleading and deceptive statements designed to fool the careless, but that Christianity on the other hand is the truth; the antithesis of deception, the right path and not a misleading one. I would certainly agree that Christianity contains the truth, but fine print does not alter truth. The deal is the deal whether you read the fine print or not. The issue of fine print is not with the claims of Christianity, but rather, with the presentation of those claims. Too often the church resorts to catchphrases and slogans, to elementary truths over spiritually mature ones, to rhetoric over reason, and concise responses instead of complete answers. The danger of this is that the church may become nothing more than a peddler of platitudes. We have already begun to see the influence and relevance of Christianity diminish in much of the Western world, in part, it seems, because people are looking for answers that are deeper than what can fit on a bumper sticker.

The reduction of robust Christian theology to a series of pithy statements may aid in the marketing of Christianity but it hinders our understanding of it. Such practices often distort the faith and lead to poor exegesis, selective presentations of the character of God, and flat out mischaracterizations of the Christian life. With such a framework, disappointment with Christ and Christianity is almost unavoidable. A day may come in the Christian life where the wind will blow and the road will be rocky, and if all we have are Christian platitudes to answer, then we will most certainly feel like everyone who doesn't bother to read the fine print. Cheated. Snookered. At that point our faith may fail, and we may become disillusioned with Christianity.

The reality is, Christianity is difficult. The God we serve is hard to follow and hard to understand; and at times the truths inherent in Scripture do not seem to coincide with the way the world is. There is a reluctance to say such a thing, not only due to fear of discouraging believers, but also out of fear that nonbelievers and antagonistic atheists might seize upon such a statement as an admission of a failed and false religion. That is certainly a possibility, but if they wish to mistake nuance for nonsense and complexity for artifice, that is their mistake to make, not ours. We should not dilute the truth of Christianity for the sensitive tastes of the nonbeliever, nor caricature God for the appeasement of the atheist.

It should be noted that I am not suggesting that we do away with tact. There is a season for everything, and in our teaching, preaching, and sharing we must be mindful of our audience. Christ said, "I have much more to say to you, more than you can now bear. But when he, the Spirit of truth, comes, he will guide you into all truth" (John 16:12–13). Jesus was very much aware of the hearts and minds of his audience, and he intentionally spoke in perplexing parables without even bothering to explain them, but simply stated, "He who has ears, let him hear" (Matt 13:9). It is not necessary, nor is it advisable to tell the exhaustive truth to those who are not ready to hear it. But that should not be an excuse to settle for truisms, lest we begin to worship a shell of the true God and follow a shadow of the true Christ.

The most foolish thing a finite mind could think is that it can know everything there is to know about an infinite subject. We must continually strive to know God better, and be prepared to cast aside our shallow mottos and mantras for real meaning. This book aims to help uncover the real deal behind common Christian bywords, and the verity underlining the Christian veneer, with every confidence that our God can stand against all scrutiny. In Christ we will not be disappointed, but will find richness and fullness we had not known; this is the fine print of Christianity.

1

Jesus Loves You: But He'll Cast You To Hell

"Jesus loves you," is often the first lesson we learn at church. It is a wonderful expression with a profoundness that I doubt any of us fully perceives. It is probably the most common dictum of all Christianity; we speak of it often, and delight in sharing it. It is a sentiment for almost every season. It can be a comfort for those experiencing a loss, an encouragement for those facing a challenge, a conviction for those doing wrong, and an instigation for worship. But in our exuberance for the axiom, and the doctrine behind it, there is a danger that we at times blithely blurt it without any consideration for context. It can quite easily be not only the first lesson, but also the only lesson taught. There are many in our culture that were brought to church in their early years, have subsequently drifted away, and now vaguely remember being taught that Jesus loves them. There are also churches that seem to only offer an elementary curriculum, and never move beyond "Jesus loves you."

It is good to know that God loves you; it is bad to know nothing else. Extrapolating from only one fact will inevitably lead to faulty conclusions. For instance, let us suppose that a man loves a dog. From this one fact we might extrapolate that the man feeds the dog, plays with it, walks it, grooms it, and perhaps even disciplines it. If he truly loves the dog, we may conclude that he would never intentionally harm or hurt the dog, but rather, will always look after the dog's best interests. Many of the inferences we have made from our one fact may be sound, but from the one fact we would never suppose that the man would throw the dog out, or even more jarring, kill it. But of course, in reality, the man who loves his dog may get rid of it in an instant if his wife is severely allergic to it. The man who loves his dog may, without any qualms whatsoever, put the dog down if ever the dog attacked his child. Contrary to our expectations and conclusions, the man might, absolutely, intentionally harm and hurt the dog. To predict and understand the man's behavior requires additional facts. Shock and surprise are derived from ignorance. If the only fact you have is that Jesus loves you unconditionally whether you do good or evil, then the facts of Hell and damnation will seem utterly out of place. If we are taken aback that Jesus, who loves us, condemns people to Hell, it is because we do not know him. More specifically, we do not know what he loves most.

The main problem is that we fixate on only one, and perhaps minute, object of God's love: ourselves. I have been told that if I were the only one on Earth, Jesus would still die for me. It is a pleasant thought, but I have no idea how anyone could know that, and I have even less an idea as to how that could possibly be demonstrated. For our purposes, let us try to stick with what we know, and avoid any thinking that could be merely wishful. What I do know is that Jesus died for me, and he did so because he loves me, but not *only* me. Even if I were the only being in the world, I would not be the only thing that God loves. We are sometimes so self-absorbed that we think God's love for us is his most important love, mainly because it is the most relevant to us. Such egocentricity can find appropriate expression, it is the reason we study Earth far more than any other planet or object in the universe. Indeed the Earth is important, but thinking it is the *most* important thing in the universe simply because it is the most personally relevant has led to some bad theories in physics. Jesus loving us is important, but thinking his love for us is of first importance leads to bad theology.

Whenever our loves are in conflict, whenever one love begins to impede another, we are forced to make a choice. If one love is permitted to thwart another, it is because the former is regarded as more precious than the latter. If, on the other hand, the former is quelled, it is because the latter has proved more valuable. Of course this only pertains to loves that are in conflict. If the wife is never allergic to the dog, then there is no reason the man cannot live with both and love both. If all our loves are at peace, we are the happier for it, but when one love disrupts another, we must and always will, turn to what is loved most. This does not make our love insincere; ridding the dog for the sake of the wife does not mean the dog is not loved, it simply means the wife is loved more, and deservedly so. If sincerity is the issue, then we must realize that to be sincere about our prime love necessitates that all other loves be subordinate to it. I think this is something of what Jesus meant when he very harshly said, "If anyone comes to me and does not hate his father and mother, his wife and children, his brothers and sisters—yes, even his own life—he cannot be my disciple" (Luke 14:26).

It is often thought that love and hate are incompatible, and Christians are sometimes labeled hypocrites because they claim to love but "preach hate." This is a gross misunderstanding. Hate is not only compatible with love, but love, being love, necessitates hate for that which is antithetical to the beloved. If you truly love righteousness, you must, necessarily, hate unrighteousness. If you love justice, you must hate injustice. If you love truth, you must hate lies. The accusation that Christians preach hate is true, only to the extent that they preach an authentic love. Ironically, the Christian who claims to love but does not hate what is in direct opposition to the beloved *is* a hypocrite. Of course Jesus' words must be interpreted in the broader context; after all, this is coming from the same man who told us to love even our enemies. But if we are hoping to remove the sting from his statements, I am afraid that we cannot; it is harsh, it is intended to be. Jesus is demanding that he and the Father be our prime loves, and thus, all other loves must be subordinate. All other loves must be tossed aside if they ever oppose our love for him. The dictum that Jesus prescribes is not made out of vain conceit or egoism, but rather, mere sensibility. It would make no sense for a man to rush the family photos out of a burning building while leaving the family among the blazes. We would either argue that he hates his family, in which case, why would he save their likeness? Or more probable, we would conclude that he is a complete fool who lacks the judgment to see what is truly valuable. God is no fool, he does not cherish what is not worth cherishing, he does not mistake rocks for diamonds. God cannot tell us that there is something better, and greater, and more satisfying than he because it is simply not true. He is the creator of the entire universe, whatever is rightly lovable in it is derived from love himself, and whatever is good in it, comes from good himself. To have greater love for something other than he is to love something lesser. It is very much like preferring the family photos to the family itself. Surely the value of the photo lies only in the greater value of its subject. The photos are images of something greater than itself, and all noble subjects loved in the world are mere images of a greater subject. In this way, it is mere sensibility and not egoism for God to tell us to value what is most valuable.

A possible protest might be made in objectively declaring God to be the most valuable. Our experiences suggest that value is subjective; as they say, one man's trash is another man's treasure. Isn't God's decree that we love him best, like a galled parent who forces the child to play with an expensive toy, rather than the packaging she prefers? If God is not egotistical perhaps he is priggish; frowning down on us like snobby critics frown at the poor taste of the masses. But to love and value God supremely is not a mere matter of taste but is a moral imperative. For God is the very manifestation of goodness, and holiness, and righteousness, and justness. A man who loathes carrots distastes only a vegetable, but a man who loathes God distastes righteousness. Preference and taste are no longer relative the moment they become moral.

A morality that is relative is no morality at all. Taste then, cannot be applied to morality precisely because morality is objective. If a man has a taste and a love for torturing infants we would rightly still condemn such a man. Even in a relativistic society such as ours, we still recognize that a person's taste becomes unacceptable and condemnable the moment it becomes immoral. Taste and preference only really apply to the trivial and the morally innocuous.

Due to God's intrinsic character, it is impossible to not love God and still be moral. Loving God is not a matter of taste, because loving God is a moral imperative. It is morally obligatory for us to love righteousness and justice, and goodness and holiness, and if we have no love for those things we are immoral. But God is the very embodiment of those qualities, and so to have no love for him is immoral for the same reason. Since God is the very embodiment of what is moral to love, if we love what is right, we ought to love him supremely.

We have traveled through some rather murky waters of philosophy, of which, I am not the best guide. But it is necessary to establish that God's importance, preciousness, and value is objective. Although value can be a projected trait, and not necessarily an inherent one, there is still objectivity, in that *morality* is objective and not subject to preference or taste. The qualities of God are inseparable with the morally good, and so to not love his qualities is immoral. We can now safely say that God is not being egotistical or pretentious in decreeing that we love and value him the most; he is merely being moral. For his very nature is inextricable from what is righteous and therefore to be moral is to love him supremely.

What is good for the goose is good for the gander. If it is sensible for us to love and value God most, then it is sensible for God to do so as well. Divine wisdom knows well where to place prime love. God loves himself most for he is the most worthy of love. Initially it may unnerve our self-esteem that we are not God's first love, that is, until we realize that if we were, it would render God a dunce and undermine the very significance of his love. The very greatness of man is accredited to being fashioned in the image of God (Gen 1:26). Should we really expect God to love the image more than the thing itself? Is he really such a fool? A god that does not recognize his prime importance in relation to his *own* creation is, to put it bluntly, a stupid god, and why should we care that a stupid god loves us? In trying to bolster ourselves, we destroy the value of God's love, and subsequently, demean our own worth. For if human worth is found in being image-bearers, it is to our own degradation that we belittle the greatness of the image we bear. The significance of Jesus loving us rests solely on who Jesus is.

God, being no fool, loves himself foremost. As we have said, whenever our loves are diametrically opposed, we always ally with the greater love. God's supreme love for himself compels him to reject all that conflicts with who he is, and to spurn all that is not at peace with his character, that is, his righteousness, holiness, justness, and goodness. It is for this reason that God is adamantly against sin, for all sin is an affront to what is most precious and loved by God. All sin is unrighteous and he is righteous, all sin is evil and he is good, all sin is death and he is life, and all the ways of sin are lies, and he is truth. If you have ever wondered why God seems to take sin so darn personally, it is because it *is* personal.

From the Scriptures we know that "all have sinned and fall short of the glory of God" (Rom 3:23), so we who sin and are in sin must be antagonists of God's prime love. In an attempt to shirk our sins, we may ask, why should such a vast God care about the actions of such trivial creatures on a tiny speck of a planet in an infinitesimal galaxy of the universe? The greater God is, we may reason, the greater his indifference for us must be. From the view of a skyscraper, man seems insignificant, how much more so from the view of God? The goal of this ruse is to put as much distance from God and ourselves as possible, so that we may find safe haven for our sin. Either God is too big and too great to notice or care about our sin, or, like an allergic man is at peace with a pet in another country, God is too far from our sin for it to be an affront. But the fault of this thinking is that it correlates greatness with apathy, and misapplies spatiality to spirit. Thinking of God in spatial terms will lead us to believe that the bigger God is, the further removed from us he must be. But God is not *big*, he is *omnipresent*, he is not spatial, he is spirit, he is not distant, he is near. There is no place conceivable where sin can exist, and not be an affront to God. There is no distance from omnipresence, or concealment from omniscience. If we are thinking that God does not notice our blemishes because he is too far above us, we are greatly mistaken. Nor does God's greatness make him indifferent. Man is greater than a molecule and grander than a virus, but that does not render him apathetic when a virus infects his beloved. Though it is true that we are lowly compared to God that does not make him apathetic when we attack his beloved. He notices, he cares, and there can be no peace in it.

The primary and authentic love God has for himself demands a resolute hate of sin, which by nature is in opposition to his cardinal love. Consistently, God ardently defends the rights due his prime love. "For my own sake," he says. "For my own sake, I do this. How can I let myself be defamed? I will not yield my glory to another" (Isa 48:11). One of the earliest names God ascribes himself is Jealous. He says, "Do not worship any other god, for the LORD, whose name is Jealous, is a jealous God" (Exod 34:14). With a righteous jealousy God acts to quash all that attempts to thwart his first love, and sometimes, in terrifying ways. He says, "I will bring distress on the people and they will walk like blind men, because they have sinned against the LORD. Their blood will be poured out like dust and their entrails like filth. Neither their silver nor their gold will be able to save them on the day of the LORD'S wrath. In the fire of his jealousy the whole world will be consumed, for he will make a sudden end of all who live in the earth" (Zeph 1:17–18). And yet God loves you, who happen to live on the earth that God will consume with a jealous fire. Right?

Indeed, God does love you, and that is never more clearly demonstrated than through Jesus. The Scriptures say, "This is love: not that we loved God, but that he loved us and sent his Son as an atoning sacrifice for our sins" (1 John 4:10). God was not content to allow those he loved to remain as enemies to him and his principal love. With humility, Jesus came, and came on behalf of you, to be scorned, ridiculed, beaten, broken, and put to death so that there might be reconciliation between you and God, and peace between his most cherished love and his love for you. "Once you were alienated from God and were enemies in your minds because of your evil behavior. But now he has reconciled you by Christ's physical body through death to present you holy in his sight" (Col 1:21–22). But understand, this is not a technicality; God did not hoodwink love of himself by dying for you. It is so very important that God loves himself chiefly, because out of his love of himself comes his love for us. What is most precious to God is what motivates him. Jesus would not have died for you if he did not love goodness. He would not have died for you if he did not love justice. He would not have died for you if he did not love grace. He would not have died for you if he did not love, love. In short, God would not have died for you if he did not love himself. Whatever benefits there are in being loved by God spring from who he is.

To understand Hell and damnation requires a proper understanding of Jesus' love for us. God's love of us stems from his deserved, proper, and appropriate prime love of himself. Such love is not derived from egoism or narcissism but is grounded in the exceeding worth of whom God is. And because he loves sincerely, he must hate what is antithetical to the beloved, all that stands in opposition to his eternal quality, what we call sin.

There is of course a distinction between sin and sinner, for although a sinner is at odds with God, God and sinners are not mutually exclusive as sin and God are. It is not contradictory to love sinners and hate sin; our own experiences attest to that. If we have had any relationship, it should be abundantly evident that it is possible (and common) to love someone and not always love what they do. Even the worst of sinners is comprised of more than just sin; if nothing else, they are still fashioned in the image of God. And to whatever extent God's image endures in man, God must surely love. But God's love does not make us immune to judgment and condemnation. We cannot use God's love as a fortress to protect our sin, for God's love of righteousness is greater than his love for us, and if we refuse to be reconciled with his prime love, he will throw us out. Any sincere lover would do likewise.

If there is any lingering doubt as to the compatibility between a God who loves and a God who condemns, listen to these words. "As surely as I live, declares the Sovereign LORD, I take no pleasure in the death of the wicked, but rather that they turn from their ways and live.

Turn! Turn from your evil ways! Why will you die, O house of Israel?" (Ezek 33:11). These are not the words of an apathetic God. In his voice there is a groaning for his people whom he loves, and who adamantly and repeatedly refuse to be reconciled with God's love. "O Jerusalem, Jerusalem, you who kill the prophets and stone those sent to you, how often I have longed to gather your children together, as a hen gathers her chicks under her wings, but you were not willing" (Matt 23:37). Heaven and Hell come to us as a choice. Do we choose to ally ourselves with Satan and sin, to the antithetical of God's beloved, and so forever remain irreconcilable? Or, do we choose to fall at the foot of the cross and be reconciled to God, and there, enter into the fullness of his love? This is the choice before all men; we cannot be in sin and be at peace with God, we cannot violate God's supreme love and expect no repercussions. God loves you, but he loves himself more. If you are unwilling to come to the one who calls, God will never choose you and deny himself. He will not choose you and deny justice and he will not choose you and deny holiness, for these are the qualities of he who is his most precious love. He will not choose you and deny his first love.

The doctrine of Hell is of course unpleasant, but the fact that it is unpleasant does not make it untrue, nor does it make it incompatible with a loving God. It simply makes it unpleasant. We earlier stated that there is no place where sin can exist and not be an affront to God. As such, there is no possibility that God could simply let us be, for he cannot tolerate sin to continue because his love of himself (and thus his hatred of sin) is sincere. He is therefore compelled to do something about sin, and us, the instruments and instigators of sin. One such response God has taken to sin is what we call Hell. This is not God's preferred option, as the Bible says God does not want "anyone to perish, but everyone to come to repentance" (2 Pet 3:9), but Hell is a necessary option, for not everyone will come.

There are essentially two arguments against the notion of Hell; the first, we have been dealing with in this chapter, is that Hell is contradictory to God's love. I hope by now we are in agreement that this is not contradictory, so long as we are not God's prime love, and as long as we are at odds with said love. The second argument is that Hell is contradictory to God's justice. I am tempted to leave this challenge for the next chapter where we will talk extensively about God's justice but I am forced to face it now as it is relevant to the question of God's love, for justice is a component of God's character, and so it is an element of his prime love. If God loves himself, he must love justice; if God loves us, he must be just to us.

If we are to effectively assail the doctrine of Hell we must take the Christian claim at face value, otherwise we are arguing against a straw man. The claim is that all of us are sinners and that it is righteous for God to condemn sinners to Hell, for sin is of such a quality that it warrants such a punishment. It is not the simple notion of Hell that is loathsome; it is actually quite pleasant to think that certain evildoers will be punished for their misdeeds. In fact, many of us would even be comfortable with our own wrongdoings receiving a slap on the wrist from a cosmic judge. The real egregious element of Hell is its severity, or I should say, its perceived severity. For to say that the punishment of Hell is too severe is to say that sin is less severe. God seems to disagree, and we have no real means of refuting him. All we can really say is that this *feels* too severe, which is truly no evidence at all; after all, the most despicable of men are the ones who do not realize they are despicable. There have surely been many who have gone unrepentant and unashamed all the way to the gas chamber, should it be so different all the way to Hell? Perhaps it is different, but the point is, you do not need to know you are wrong to be wrong, nor do you need to acknowledge justice for justice to be done.

Still, I do not want to simply ignore our feelings on the severity of Hell, for many of our feelings are confirmed by God to be accurate. Perhaps we should examine what specifically about Hell we find to be too severe. In dealing with Hell, it should be noted that the Bible provides very few details, and much discussion on the subject is mere conjecture. We can, however, glean a couple of concepts from Scripture. The first, and perhaps most despised, is that Hell is everlasting. Jesus said that the condemned will "go away to eternal punishment, but the righteous to eternal life" (Matt 25:46). There are also numerous references to an eternal fire. "Depart from me, you who are cursed, into the eternal fire prepared for the devil and his angels" (Matt 25:41) and again, "be thrown into hell, where 'their worm does not die, and the fire is not quenched.' Everyone will be salted with fire" (Mark 9:47–49). If God truly loves us, and does not delight in punishing the wicked as he says, then why is the punishment so severe? Does it not seem disproportionate to punish momentary sins for eternity? Part of the problem is that it is very difficult for a finite mind to wrap itself around an eternal subject. I have the suspicion that when we speak *duration* in regards to eternity, we are talking utter nonsense. Eighty years incarceration is a severe sentence to us, but isn't that only because the entire lifespan of a human is not much more than that? If the average lifespan of a human were five thousand years, would eighty years still be sufficient for heinous crimes? Probably not. Now let us suppose that man is an everlasting being. How many years would be sufficient to punish monstrous acts committed by an everlasting being? It does not seem possible to punish everlasting beings with time, and so the question of how long they will be punished, is if not complete nonsense, irrelevant. The only relevant question becomes whether the punishment they receive befits the crime.

It is not clear what the punishment fully entails. Fire, darkness, isolation, imprisonment, and even physical beatings are some of the haunting imagery conjured of Hell. But we should be cautious how much we read into such visual language because it is not evident that such pictures should be taken literally. What is evident is that the imagery of Hell is ghastly, because the punishment of Hell is ghastly; there is little else we can say with confidence on the matter. Though the nature of the punishment is ambiguous, there is an indication that it will not be entirely uniform, but rather, will have varying degrees. "That servant who knows his master's will and does not get ready or does not do what his master wants will be beaten with many blows. But the one who does not know and does things deserving punishment will be beaten with few blows" (Luke 12:47–48). Jesus further says to the cities of Korazin and Bethsaida, "it will be more bearable for Tyre and Sidon on the day of judgment than for you" (Matt 11:22).

The final notion invoked of Hell is one of destruction. "By the same word," says the Apostle Peter, "the present heavens and earth are reserved for fire, being kept for the day of judgment and destruction of ungodly men" (2 Pet 3:7). The Bible further states that the condemned "will be punished with everlasting destruction" (2 Thess 1:9), and that "their destiny is destruction" (Phil 3:19). It may seem a bit odd to meld the concept of an eternal punishment with that of destruction, but their fusion might lend some insight into our loving God. Again, we must be mindful that detailed discussion of Hell contains a good deal of speculation, but if destruction is a component of judgment, it is well worth asking, what exactly is destroyed? It cannot be the total self; annihilation simply cannot coincide with eternal punishment. It may be helpful to look at it in another way. Heaven is a nice contrast to Hell. We are told that those who are in Christ are a new creation and when at long last we stand before God the last remnant of our sinful nature will perish and we will be fully sanctified, remade in perfection and glory (2 Cor 5:17). If the believer is made fit for Heaven, perhaps the nonbeliever is rendered fit for Hell. At judgment, God gives to the believer regeneration, and to the nonbeliever, degeneration. Perhaps what is destroyed is the last remains of God's image, the last element of what made them lovable. It might be possible to say that though still recognizable, we do not really know anyone in Hell. If you will pardon a crude analogy, it is almost like the walking dead. Shadows of their former selves, more monster than man, turned over completely to their sinful nature, they are reduced to nothing but objects of wrath, forever remaining restless, and in misery, consciously suffering, trapped in their evil and never repenting.[1] This is just postulation, but perhaps, the conflict between Jesus loving and condemning people to Hell is more easily resolved than we think. Jesus may cease to love you when, by your own choice, you cease to be what he loved.

The doctrine of Jesus' love is pleasant, the doctrine of damnation is not, and I cannot make it pleasant. But we cannot and should not ignore it. The best we can do is to try to understand it better, and dedicate ourselves to deciphering the wondrous intricacies of a God who both loves and condemns. If we choose to reject the only means of our reconciliation and ally ourselves with sin and all such antagonists of God's first love, we must expect that a God of deep, authentic love will, with righteous jealousy, destroy that which assails his love. That is the very nature of love, and that is the nature of God.

---

1. When referring to the damned as being "evil" and turned over to their "sin nature" I am not proposing that they continue to sin, though some theologians have argued that. The continual presence of sin must be a continual affront to God's prime love and I do not think he will tolerate that. It is not that they continue to transgress, but that they must live with the effects of their transgressions, absent of the grace of God. A rabid smoker who has not touched a cigarette in years might still suffer from a nasty cough all the days of his life, and the damned need not continue to sin to continually suffer the effects of sin. And the effect of sin is death, everlasting destruction.

2

God Is Just: But Life's Not Fair

IT IS NOT A new phenomenon. Sickness, corruption, pain, suffering, disaster, sin, and wickedness permeate all of human history, and present us with an inescapable sense that the world is not as it should be. Moral men are mocked while the immoral are propelled to stardom and fame. Hurricanes rip through churches and Christ-centered homes, while leaving districts of debauchery intact. God-fearing couples are told they are infertile while millions of mothers kill their own babies. It is not hard to feel, as did the author of Ecclesiastes, that "in the place of judgment—wickedness was there, in the place of justice—wickedness was there" (Eccl 3:16). And upon seeing this, we might ask along with Jeremiah, "Why does the way of the wicked prosper? Why do all the faithless live at ease?" (Jer 12:1), or complain like Habakkuk, "How long, O Lord, must I call for help, but you do not listen? Or cry out to you, 'Violence!' but you do not save? Why do you make me look at injustice? Why do you tolerate wrong?" (Hab 1:2–3). It is not a new phenomenon.

And yet, God is just; parents and pastors, churches and books have told us so. Even a cursory glance over the Bible will reveal bold claims that "he is the Rock, his works are perfect, and all his ways are just" (Deut 32:4), and that "righteousness and justice are the foundation of [his] throne" (Ps 89:14). We are not being lied to; God is just, even in a world where bad things happen to good people and good things happen to bad people. But we cannot simply rest here, acknowledging that God is just while perceiving the world to be utterly unjust, and chalk it up to "God's mysterious ways." Do not mistake faithfulness with thoughtlessness. The kingdom of heaven is not comprised of pat answers, but profound ones. We must earnestly seek to understand God's justice and endeavor to answer the tough questions.

Why in fact *do* bad things happen to good people, and good things happen to bad people? In answering this there is something very important to notice. In order to pose the question, a judgment must already be rendered. You must have already judged by some standard who is "good," who is "bad," and that what they have received is "bad" or "good." I said "in fact," but in reality it may not be a fact at all, unless the standard that is used to measure goodness and badness is itself factual. The world will absolutely seem topsy-turvy if we are standing on our heads, but we would be very foolish to think that everything is *actually* upside down. We must be standing upright to get an accurate reading. In the same way, when we judge "goodness" and "badness" we need to be sure that we are standing upright in order for the argument to carry any weight.

From the Christian viewpoint (and in this book we will always be using the Christian view), God is the standard for how we measure good and evil. God is good and anything that is in opposition to him is evil. It is important to notice that when we say that God is good, we do not mean that God is behaving well. God is not acting goodly, he is not living up to some external standard of good; God *is* the standard. There is nothing above God. Goodness is his nature, not simply his behavior. This is very important because it serves as the foundation for our understanding of goodness.

We tend to think that goodness is a matter of degree. For instance, we might feel that God is 100 percent good, and we are perhaps 75 percent good, and therefore we are, overall, good. But remember: God's goodness is his nature, and nature is not a matter of degree. God is good in the same way that humans are mammals. Thinking we are 75 percent good is as nonsensical as a fish thinking it is 75 percent mammal. You are either a mammal or you are not, you are either good or you are not; there is no degree. Water that is comprised of 25 percent or even 10 percent salt would never be regarded as being fresh water overall. Anyone with any sense would spit out all water that was not fresh.

If we are to judge our goodness with any relevance, we must judge it in comparison to God, for God is the standard. As the tuning fork is the measurement for pitch, God is the measurement for goodness. God is good by nature; he is intrinsically good as the tuning fork is intrinsically in tune. If we are to call ourselves good we must be completely in tune with him. Being 75 percent on pitch means nothing.

What, then, is the nature of man? Do we have perfect pitch? Are we, by our nature, good, as God is in his nature? Another cursory glance through the Bible will definitively answer that question with a resounding no. Jesus said, "No one is good—except God alone" (Mark 10:18), and the Apostle Paul concludes from Scripture that no one will be declared righteous for, "there is no one righteous not even one," and again, "there is no one who does good, not even one" (Rom 3:10–12). Isaiah declares, "All of us have become like one who is unclean" (Isa 64:6), and David writes in the Psalms, "no one living is righteous before [God]" (Ps 143:2). Of the heart of man it says, "the heart is deceitful above all things and beyond cure" (Jer 17:9), and that we are, "by nature objects of wrath" (Eph 2:3). Man, by nature, is not good. In essence then, a "bad" thing happening to a "good" man is not a possibility, as there are no good men by God's standard. So is our argument against God's justice in shambles? Not quite.

There is a second component to the argument. It is not simply that bad things happen to good people but that *good* things happen to *bad* people. We are not comparing ourselves to God, in which case no one would be counted as good; we are comparing ourselves to each other. Now this might be very confusing after what we have just talked about. After all, if we use the same analogy, is any fish more or less mammal than another fish? Is there any sense in comparing ourselves? There is a good deal of sense in it, because there is a difference between nature and behavior. Jesus plainly says that we are evil, but that we can, and do, "give good gifts to [our] children" (Luke 11:13). Although we are not good in nature, it is certainly possible to act contrary to our nature, and to do good. For instance, it is not natural for a dog to shake hands, or heel, or follow auditory commands; a wild dog would not do such things. If left to its own nature, a dog would never behave in the manner of a domesticated animal. When a human teaches a dog to shake, he impresses upon the dog something that is not intrinsic to the dog. Men greet one another with handshakes, dogs don't. Whenever we train or teach a dog, we are imprinting in them human behaviors or expectations. In the same way, although we are not by nature good, God impresses upon us his goodness. In this way, the one who obeys God is good, just as the dog that obeys his master is good. But please understand, the fact that we can do good does not make our nature good, anymore than training a dog makes it more than an animal.

We may all be mutts, but some of us obey the master, and some of us do not, and in that sense, some of us *are* better than others. If we are all equally bad, both in nature and behavior, then we should expect equal treatment. However, if we are not equal in behavior, and it seems that we are not, it is then reasonable to assume that those who obey the master should receive better treatment than those who disobey. But from our vantage, that is not always the case. That is the very reason the prophets were complaining. People do not always seem to get what they deserve. And if people are not getting what they deserve then how is God just?

At this point, it would be prudent to define our terms. What exactly is justice? Often when we think of justice, we think in terms of just deserts. When we see a car recklessly speeding, we are filled with a sense of jubilation when we spot that same car a few miles ahead, pulled over by the highway patrol. "Justice is served," we might say, or "he got what he had coming to him." Now, the sense of glee we experience can be a very twisted thing, where we are rejoicing not in justice, but in the suffering and misfortunes of others. Even so, when the gavel hits we generally want the sentence to be what the defendant deserves, whether it be freedom or chains. Justice then, from a worldly perspective, is the dispensing of what is deserved, whether what is deserved is good or ill.

This idea certainly has merit, and we are generally quite comfortable with it, but when we begin to apply it to Christianity it becomes increasingly uncomfortable. "Eye for an eye and tooth for a tooth" is a very welcome sentiment, but the Christ of Christianity shatters it (Matt 5:38–39). For at the heart of Christianity is a sort of great injustice; an innocent man is put to death for crimes he did not commit, while the guilty party is set free.

You may now see why our thinking of justice is a bit inadequate. If justice is merely the getting of what we deserve then mercy is a subversion of justice and grace a perversion. Yet God, whom we rightly say is just, is also merciful and gracious. We should not think that God is, with one hand, covering his eyes to justice, while with the other, dispensing grace and mercy. God is not divided amongst himself for we know that a house divided against itself cannot stand (Mark 3:25). We must then conclude that grace and mercy are not operating under the radar of God's justice, but rather that they are enacted by it. In that case, our idea of justice needs some revision.

If we think properly about justice, we should see that justice is not so much concerned with what is deserved, but rather, with what is right, or, to use more spiritual terminology, with what is righteous. Justice is the administration of righteousness. With this understanding, mercy and grace are no longer antagonists of justice, but instruments of it, in the same way that punishment is an instrument of justice. In fact, with Calvary we see retribution, mercy, and grace all exemplified in the crucifixion. It was righteous for God to punish sin, just as it was righteous for God to save people from their sins.

I sense that there is a hesitancy to embrace such a view. So strong is our conviction in just deserts that the idea of people not getting what they deserve is repulsive. Receiving mercy and grace instead of the punishment that is deserved, we feel, undermines the severity of the wrongdoing. If people are not getting what they deserve, then how will they know that what they did was wrong? Not wanting God to be flippant about evil, we suppress his grace and mercy. Our feelings on this matter are understandable, however misplaced. A doctor would never refuse to treat an illness out of fear that the patient will not recognize the severity of the illness. Chances are good that the moment the patient realizes he needs medical attention, will be the very same moment he realizes the severity of the condition. In the same way, the moment we recognize mercy as mercy and grace as grace can be the very same moment we recognize our own wickedness. The truth is, we are more flippant about evil when we demand our just deserts than when we receive mercy and grace. A man who recognizes that he is living by grace will never think himself better than he is, but the man who lives by just deserts will very easily become deluded into thinking that all his blessings and even his own salvation are due to the quality of his character. Hence, a justice of mere comeuppance trivializes the corrupt nature of man and the severity of man's sin far more than mercy and grace ever could.

The simple fact is that if everyone got what he or she deserved, not one of us would enter Heaven. We want just deserts, except when it pertains to us. In trying to maintain a justice of getting what is deserved, some might argue that Jesus' death makes us worthy of Heaven, for those who believe, and therefore, people *do* get what they deserve. But in making this claim, another word has slipped in, and that is "worthy." Although "worthy" is often synonymous with "deserving," it also has another meaning. It can mean "suitable" or "good enough," and that is quite different from *deserving*. The crucifixion certainly does make us suitable for salvation, but not deserving of it, for the very simple reason that the crucifixion is an act of grace. No one can make you deserving of grace, for that is a contradiction in terms. It is for our own benefit that we leave our rigid understanding of justice behind. If grace has no place in justice, we have no place in Heaven. If mercy is abominable then our very existence must be, this instant, abolished! If God is indeed just, our only hope in the world is that our tenet of just deserts is deficient. All other comfort is illusory. Even so, there must be a reason why we feel so strongly, why we cling and hold fast to a justice, that if applied appropriately, would be detrimental to us. We are not complete madmen for doing so, for we are responding to something that has been impressed upon us by God himself: the Law.

To the Jews he gave the Law, and to the Gentiles he wrote it upon their hearts, so that "through the law we become conscious of sin" (Rom 3:20). For you can never understand grace, until you realize that you do not deserve it. God has ingrained in us a sense of justice, so that we might understand what has been revealed, a greater and fuller justice. Or as the Apostle Paul puts it, "a righteousness from God, apart from law, has been made known, to which the Law and the Prophets testify" (Rom 3:21). It is not surprising then, that Jesus was accused of being a law-breaker. Even now, we might feel a bit anxious that by affirming a justice of mercy and grace, we are nullifying the law. The Apostle Paul writes of this, and Jesus reassures us that he did not come to "abolish the Law or the Prophets," but to "fulfill them" (Matt 5:17). Rules are not rules for the mere sake of being rules. Behind them lies reason and principles. The rules of grammar, for instance, are in place to ensure that we communicate clearly and effectively. And yet, a fragment, though grammatically incorrect, can be, in the hands of one who understands the principles, a powerful tool for communicating clearly and effectively. In doing so, it breaks the rules, but honors the very reason the rules are there to begin with.

The law is but a silhouette of the face of God. But when light comes into the world, all shadows must fade. The truth we have gleaned from the silhouette is still true, but Christ has filled in what was once only an outline, and to what was flat, God has given dimension. We should not think that when light comes into the world, the world could go on exactly as it was. Though it may sting our eyes for a moment, we have seen color for the very first time, and now it is quite impossible to revert back to our grayscale. The silhouette taught us that the Lord is one, and the light has revealed that he is triune. The silhouette taught us "eye for an eye and tooth for a tooth," and the light has taught us to turn the other cheek. The Trinity does not undermine the oneness of God and turning the other cheek is not a slap in the face of justice. "Eye for an eye" and "turn the other cheek" are not contradictory, for the same principle underpins them both, and that is, righteousness. God is principled, not legalistic. Even in our own courts, the good judge is at times stern and at other times merciful. Not because he is relativistic, but because he is honoring the principle that lies behind the law itself. So terrified are we of relativism, that we bind ourselves to something absolutely rigid, and neither is just. If we deny God any flexibility in his administration of righteousness, then we have reduced him to something more akin to Victor Hugo's Inspector Javert, a character in *Les Misérables* who is so consumed with the letter of the law that he lacks all compassion, mercy, and grace. And without those tools his pursuit of justice becomes a detestable perversion of justice.

In one of Jesus' parables, a servant begs his master to be merciful, because the servant owes the master a large sum of money. The master acts in grace and cancels the whole debt. But later, that same servant goes out and is unmerciful to a fellow servant who owes him money. When the master hears of this, he throws the servant to whom he had shown mercy into jail to be tortured until he can pay back the debt (Matt 18:23–25). From this parable, was the master just in throwing the servant into jail? Was the master also just in being gracious to the servant? If you agree that he was just in both cases, then we must acknowledge that justice was served when the servant got what he deserved (prison) and when he did not get what he deserved (the debt canceled). God always does what is right because his nature is righteous, but what is right can be different for different situations. To be clear, I am not suggesting that God's justice is relative. God's justice is not relative, for his justice is based on his righteousness, and his righteousness is inherent to his character, and his character is unchanging. True relativism is arbitrary and has no grounding, but God's administration of righteousness is grounded in his character. What I am merely trying to get at is that God is righteous not *only* because he punishes unrighteousness, but also, and equally, because he redeems it.

As we have now seen, our sense of justice, of getting what is deserved, is derived from the law, which is instilled in us, so that we might be cognizant of sin, and thereby perceive mercy and grace, in order to understand through Christ a more robust justice; one which utilizes punishment, mercy, and grace at the directive of righteousness. We should now, at long last, be able to shed some light on our old question. If people are not getting what they deserve, how is God just? The once inexplicable question, now that we have walked the roundabout road, seems quite clearly the product of a muddled mind. If we are truly living by grace, we are fools to complain that people do not get what they deserve. The simple fact that bad people, those who reject the instruction of the master, receive grace does not make God unjust, for they are just the sorts of people who need grace. And the simple fact that good people receive hardships, and trials, and every kind of perceived bad thing, *also* does not make God unjust, for I suspect they are just the sorts of people who need it. In each and every circumstance, God acts righteously, but the enacting of righteousness need not be uniform. In fact, if it were uniform, it would probably be unrighteous.

Of course all of this seems to hinge on the idea that it was righteous for the bad thing to happen to the good man and that is a distasteful idea. Righteousness and badness, we reason, do not make for good allies. Perhaps we are mistaken about God's righteousness, and he is not really righteous, as we had thought. Or, we might be mistaken about the bad thing, and it is not actually bad, as we had believed. The latter is more plausible, so we will begin there. In the same way we examined the standard for judging a good man from a bad man, we must now examine the standard we employ for judging a good thing from a bad thing.

"Bad thing" is terribly nondescript, but in this instance, it is referring to negative events outside of man's control. It is not addressing the natural cause and effect of bad behavior reaping bad results, for that undercuts the character of the man as "good" and cripples the argument. Besides, we are perfectly at peace with a system of cause and effect, after all, that is the natural order of things. But when there is no discernable moral cause, when man is not in control, and not, at least not directly, responsible, all sorts of terrible things still occur. Loved ones pass away, cancer emerges, and famines, droughts, and natural disasters devastate societies. Are we really to think that these things are not actually and truly bad? To be sure, God thinks differently about what is good and what is bad than we do. As God says, "My thoughts are not your thoughts, neither are your ways my ways . . . as the heavens are higher than the earth, so are my ways higher than your ways and my thoughts than your thoughts" (Isa 55:8–9). But we are not so totally depraved or earthly-minded that our thoughts of good and evil are antithetical to God's. If they were, then all discussion of God's justice would be futile. It is sensible to think that we regard things like natural disasters as bad, not because our faculties are insufficient, or our perceptions too warped, but because natural disasters *are* bad. Again, we are speaking of natural disasters without direct moral causality. God can use any natural or supernatural force to impose his retribution, as he did with the great flood, or the angel of death passing over Egypt. These examples, and there are many others, are demonstrations of God's retributive justice: the direct effect of man's immoral behavior. But that is not what we are talking about. We are talking about the floods that kill not only the godless, but along with them the God-fearing, or more confounding, floods that kill the God-fearing but spare the godless. In these instances, behavior is not the factor, at least, not directly.

If it is not simple behavior, then nature must be the prime culprit. But as you may recall, the nature of all men is evil, so why should there be any perceived discrepancy? If God must send floods on account of our wicked nature, then why do some and not all perish? Worse still, the Scripture has told us that we who believe in Christ are a "new creation" (2 Cor 5:17) and that we are, "controlled not by the sinful nature but by the Spirit, if the Spirit of God lives in [us]" (Rom 8:9). If our behavior is better than others, and our nature is no longer of sin, but of the Spirit, then why are we still afflicted, and at times, afflicted more grievously than those who are not of the Spirit? This is a difficult question, but we compound the problem by mistakenly thinking that our nature can be treated in isolation from other natures. A snake is different in nature than a human, but you would be daft to think that means it cannot bite you. As long as the world has snakes, and snakes have teeth, they can bite you. If the world we live in is full of bad natures, we should expect bad things to occur, and we, who are a part of the world, are not immune to it. There are other natures at play. We have talked about the nature of man, now we must talk about the nature of Nature; that is, Mother Nature. The two are more connected than we typically think, for they were both determined in a garden long ago.

The Fall is a crucial doctrine of Christianity, for it tells us that what God created was originally good. The nature of man is evil, but it was not always that way. God created man good and gave to man good gifts: consciousness and free will. But inherent in those gifts is a danger. As C. S. Lewis wrote, "the moment a creature becomes aware of God as God and of itself as self, the terrible alternative of choosing God or self for the centre is opened to it."[1] And that is exactly what happened; man chose to serve his own will over God's. There can be no righteous deviation from God, for as we have repeatedly said, God *is* good, he is the track and we are the train. God has created us in his image, to be reflections of him, to be good as he is good, and in order to do that we must follow him. There is no good deviation from the track, it results in only derailment, and the train and all it carries is damaged. In this way, evil has entered the world and man's nature was corrupted, but not man's nature alone. The Scriptures indicate that all of creation fell with man, and that it, even now, waits eagerly, groaning to be restored (Rom 8:19–23). At first, this might be slightly puzzling. It is understandable that man's action would affect the nature of man, but why should it affect other natures? The simple reason is that we were not created in isolation. Creation is a system, and man an integral part. When one part goes awry, the whole system suffers. The one computer program that lets in the virus is not the only program affected. The one musician that is flat ruins the sound of the whole ensemble. The one tire that is ruptured hobbles the entire car. To man, God gave authority; he was the tender of the garden, the ruler of the animals, and the steward of all creation. A wicked king will have a wicked kingdom. Along with man, the nature of Nature became evil.

To use the familiar anthropomorphism, Mother Nature, in her former glory, was in perfect harmony with God and man, God her sovereign and we her prince. She was created to serve as the expression of all human pleasures, the delight of the senses, the satisfaction of work, and the medium for physical beings to worship, fellowship, and commune with the creator. She was a home like we have not yet known, but now she is merely a rest stop, only a place to catch our breath before we must drudge on. Her corrupt nature extends to all physical matter, down to the last molecule, down to the last atom, and brings decay, disease, and death. In the human body it may breed cancer, or senility, or frailty. In the world it may produce storms, floods, chaos, and destruction. We

---

1. Lewis, *Problem of Pain*, 70.

are not in isolation, we are not immune to other natures, and we are certainly not immune to Mother Nature. The "bad things" will happen because she is bad. We may mutter, "Why doesn't God do something about her?" There is a plan to do so, but like so many things, nature cannot be fixed while it is still running. It is in need of a hard reboot, but when that happens, whatever is not saved will be lost. God can destroy all the misery, and pain, and affliction of this world, but to do so, he must refine the world itself in fire. "But the day of the Lord will come like a thief. The heavens will disappear with a roar; the elements will be destroyed by fire, and the earth and everything in it will be laid bare" (2 Pet 3:10). God permits the cruelty of the universe, so that you and I and many others may be saved when it is judged. The wisdom of the Apostle Peter is evident when he writes, "The Lord is not slow in keeping his promise, as some understand slowness. He is patient with you, not wanting anyone to perish, but everyone to come to repentance" (2 Pet 3:9). Do not begrudge God his patience.

Fine, we may consent that God is just in allowing the evilness of all things to continue. After all, the good judge does not act rashly, but waits patiently for all the evidence to be in before rendering his verdict. Still, it may be sensible, merciful, gracious, and just for God to permit the bad natures to endure, but for the ones already saved, why are we still subject to them? Couldn't God protect us, and shield, and shelter us from all bad natures? I am not sure that he could. The man who needs and receives a new heart must at some point, regardless of duration, have no heart at all. It is not good to have a bad heart, it is worse to have no heart, but the old one must be completely removed to allow room for the new. It is not good to have a house with a shoddy foundation, it is worse to have no home at all, but in order to fix the foundation your house must be made uninhabitable. For a time, you must be homeless. We have been told that "in all things God works for the good of those who love him" (Rom 8:28), and we are horrified to find that it might actually be true. "All things," might very well mean, all things. Both good and bad natures may be used by God to remake us in perfection. The rub of perfection, in being perfection, is that nothing less can precede it. We cannot press on in our arithmetic when we have made an error at the beginning. We must erase it all and start anew. The sports team that loses a game cannot attain a perfect season, until a fresh season comes. Our fallen spirits and bodies must be disposed of completely before they can be made perfect.

We are not completely mistaken to call bad natures "bad," but to say that it is simply "bad" is myopic. It is a great paradox; persecution is bad, but Jesus calls us blessed by it; suffering is bad, but the Scriptures tell us to rejoice in them (Matt 5:11–12). God is at work in us, he is setting right our crooked nature. We may wish the process were painless, that we would be free from hardships and struggles, that we could fix our foundation without losing our home, but God knows better. "Our present sufferings are not worth comparing with the glory that will be revealed in us" (Rom 8:18). When the tawdry house is demolished, the foundation can be laid for an eternal home. When the body succumbs to death, it will be resurrected in perfection when the just God comes to judge.

What has been said of God is true: in all ways he is just. Grounded in his nature he administers righteousness, being patient and merciful when warranted, gracious when appropriate, and vengeful when required. With grace, God sent his son to an undeserving world and poured out on Christ the wrath our iniquities incurred. In patience God permits evil natures to endure so that through his mercy many more may find redemption. In those who have found salvation by God's grace, he sets to work, beginning the process of remaking us in perfection. In the hands of the great physician even evil is used to forge perfection, sometimes in pain, and sometimes in suffering, but always in ways befitting a God called just.

3

God Is The Great Physician: But Sickness and Suffering Persist

A PRAYER FOR HEALING is perhaps the most common kind of prayer heard in any given church. It seems there is always a need for it; a minor surgery here, a major one there; a small affliction one moment, a debilitating disease the next. Thankfully, the need is generally mild, and most ailments are easily treatable by skilled human hands and modern medicine. The common cold lives up to its namesake, and terminal illnesses are graciously rare. And yet, even in the few years I have been upon the earth, it is staggering how many people I have personally known, who, even now, either live with an incurable disease, or have been overcome by it. I have seen cancer of various kinds, Alzheimer's, brain damage, nerve damage, infertility, deafness, blindness, and even narcolepsy. I doubt my own experiences are particularly unique; if pressed, I am sure you could also easily produce a list of equal proportion. No, I am afraid it is not unique. In fact, it is offensively normal that many continue to suffer, sometimes grievously, while we continue to pray to a God that we are told can heal.

Just flip through the Gospels if you do not believe that God can heal. The Son of Man strolls along performing miracle after miracle, healing the sick, curing the deaf, the blind, the mute, the lepers, the paralytic, and even raising the dead! Such wondrous works are talked about frequently in Christian circles, and it is no surprise why. Second only to God's love, there is nothing more comforting to a believer than God's immense power to heal. There is no greater security than that which is in God's sovereignty, and no greater tranquility than in the knowledge that God is able. Whatever illness, struggle, or calamity may befall us, we take courage in knowing that the Great Physician is able to remedy it. But the truth is, it seems that God does not always heal. In fact, if we are being honest, it seems like God rarely heals, and so God's omnipotence brings as much confusion as comfort.

There are some who might object to my characterization of God's healing as being rare, for they attribute the work of human physicians to the Great Physician, and therefore every successful surgery or treatment is accredited to God, and you could hardly call this rare. In a sense they are right, for the ability of a doctor to heal rests solely in the power of something that no human physician is responsible for, and that is life. No matter how well you may set and cast the broken arm of a corpse, it will not mend. Physicians can heal our bodies only because living bodies already have the power to heal, and that power comes from no man. If that is what the objectors are crediting to God, I am in full agreement; the problem comes when others would argue that God is the Great Physician because he uses human physicians to do his bidding, and to fulfill his will that we should be healed. I have no doubt that God can use individuals to achieve his goals, but I feel such actions of God are not suited to the title of Great Physician, if for no other reason, because it is not consistently applied. We do not call God the Great Mechanic, even though God may use my mechanic to fix my car in order to fulfill his will that I should have a working vehicle. I do not mean to make fun, there are definitely people who are struggling financially and desperately need a functioning car, and to have their car fixed is certainly a gift from God. But when we invoke the title of Great Physician I believe we are referring to something more than mere providence. The way I am using the title is the way, I believe, it is most commonly used, when man is helpless, when modern medicine fails, when a miracle is needed. It is at those times when God's healing actions are rare.

I think the gap between a God who *can* heal, and does not seem to, is a gap in knowledge. If you have ever seen anyone go through non-emergency surgery, you will know that they look much better going in to surgery than they ever do coming out. And if you did not know any better, that is, if you did not know the *reason* for surgery, you would probably judge it to be utterly unnecessary, even barbarically *harmful*. But the knowledgeable physician understands that sometimes a painful recovery is a necessary step for a healthy life. It may very well turn out that we are groaning over the first incision that God made to save or better our lives.

Any good physician learns to recognize what is vital and what is not, and he will treat what is most important first. That is the whole premise behind triage. All of us are sensible enough to know that a brain injury is more severe than a hand injury, but between God and ourselves, there seems to be a disagreement as to what is critical and what is not. The simple fact is that God does not seem to care as much about our physical bodies as we do. "If your foot causes you to sin," says Jesus, "cut it off. It is better for you to enter life crippled than to have two feet and be thrown into hell" (Mark 9:45). We may reassure ourselves that such statements are merely hyperbole, and we would be right to do so, but it is hyperbole for a point. There is something crucial at stake, even more crucial than our own bodies. If we pause to think for a moment we will most likely concur with the Great Physician; there *is* something more critical. Our bodies are temporal, and there is something eternal. Our bodies are perishable and there is something imperishable. As the Apostle Paul writes, "I declare to you, brothers, that flesh and blood cannot inherit the kingdom of God, nor does the perishable inherit the imperishable" (1 Cor 15:50). Too often, we fix our eyes on what is seen and not what is unseen, on what is temporal and not eternal, on what is perishing and not what is imperishable. We have not thoroughly learned triage.

God is always at work in the believer: healing, shaping, and refashioning us for our eternal bodies and everlasting dwelling. It is to this that God most often turns as we wail and fixate on what will inevitably pass away. But this raises another question: Is God such a being that his attention cannot be divided? Shouldn't an omnipotent, omniscient being, be able to multitask? If God is at work on my soul, very good, but shouldn't God be able to heal my physical body at the same time? Triage is an insufficient answer, for it is only used when you have more wounds than capable hands to heal, and that cannot possibly be attributed to an omnipotent God.

In the previous chapter I made the rather irksome claim that God is just in permitting pain and suffering to endure, because it is necessary, and even *good* for us. It is not a happy point, but I think it is a valid one, and it is relevant to the issue at hand. If we are wondering why God cannot simultaneously remake our souls and heal the painful suffering of our bodies, it is because God is *using* the pain and suffering of our bodies *to* remake our souls. This is his instrument.

The Apostle Paul, more irksome than I, says that we should even, "rejoice in our sufferings, because we know that suffering produces perseverance; perseverance, character; and character, hope" (Rom 5:3-4). It is an odd thing that character should produce hope, but it is exactly right, for through our suffering and perseverance we are being remade into a new creation. And that rejuvenation, or change in character, bears witness to the transformational power of the living Christ. This testifies to the truth that Jesus Christ is risen, and that we shall rise with him to a world without suffering and a body without pain. And we are filled with hope.

Now, it is one thing to say that pain and suffering is useful, it is another thing to say that it is necessary. Why must we be subject to such a process? After all, even the Scripture says, "in a flash, in the twinkling of an eye," we will be, "raised imperishable, and will be changed" (1 Cor 15:52). If such a dramatic and complete transformation can take place in the "twinkling of an eye," why must we endure the suffering of such a slow and grinding process? Would it not be better if those who came to believe in Christ were instantaneously transformed in glory and perfection? While this is a very nice thought, if pain and suffering is really the main issue, perfection cannot save you. Jesus was perfect when Lazarus died. Jesus was perfect when he was betrayed. Jesus was perfect when his friends abandoned him, perfect when he was mocked, perfect when he was beaten, and perfect when he was put to death. As I said before, yours is not the only nature at play. So long as imperfect natures remain, suffering and pain can and will afflict even the perfect.

While it is true perfection cannot in itself protect you from pain and suffering, astute readers will realize that our problem still remains. I earlier argued that God does not shield us from pain and suffering because God is using it to remake us in perfection. But if perfection can be achieved instantaneously, then there is seemingly no reason for pain and suffering, and therefore no reason why God could not or maybe should not protect us from enduring it. To put it simply, if God has the ability, why don't we just skip all the unpleasantness and get to the end result? Part of the answer is that to forgo the process of sanctification for the results of sanctification seems very much like pinning medals worthy of war heroes onto a soldier who has never been near a battle. There is something to be said for the *experience*, not just the final outcome. We would probably agree that our experiences, whether painful or not, have helped to shape and even define who we are. You might even say that those experiences are *necessary* for creating the very specific sort of being that is you, and without those experiences, you would not be you. The fully sanctified man will be perfect, not bland. There is no reason to think that the new creation will not be every bit as diverse as the old. Entailed in this wondrous variety is the unique creation of you and me, creatures fashioned by God into very specific sorts of beings, by our very particular experiences. You would not be the sort of new being that God has in mind if you did not have the particular experiences that make up that new being.

I do not see that it is possible for God to instantaneously remake you in perfection, if a main ingredient in your remaking is an experience you have in time. To have an authentic experience, you must, in actuality, *experience* it. You must go through it. An illustration might help here. Let us suppose that there was a perfect clone of you created instantaneously. And let us suppose that it was identical to you in all respects: it looked like you, talked like you, thought like you, and had all of your memories and knowledge of all the particular experiences that make up you. Even with such perfect duplication, there would still be a fundamental difference between you and the clone. The memories and the experiences of the clone are not real. They are contrary to reality, and the clone is nothing more than a forgery. God does not deal in forgeries. He does not make prefect beings by filling their heads with lies. If God is to create a particular sort of authentic being, that new being must have the proper sorts of experiences conducive for its creation.

This is also the reason we should not compare our own hardships with another's. I can speak for myself that it is sometimes frustrating to watch others seemingly prance through life with ease, while I perceive my own life to be plagued with troubles, trials, and all sorts of unpleasantness. At such moments, it is tempting to complain to God that my suffering is too much or has gone on too long. But on what basis can I legitimately say that? Unless I know exactly what kind of creature God is fashioning me to be, my protest of too much suffering is rather like complaining to a chef that he is using too much salt without having the foggiest idea what sort of dish he is preparing. Upon reflection, I am forced to confess that I have no idea what the recipe is for preparing the new creation that is to be me. I do not know what sort of seasoning sufferings are required or how long I must marinate in them. What is known is that I am not you, and you are not I, we are being prepared differently because we are different. It does us no good to compare ourselves to one another in that way, for we are the proverbial apples and oranges.

When we toil and suffer, we may wish that God would have another sort of creation in mind for us, but that is wishing to be a lesser being. For it is to our future glory that we suffer, "for our light and momentary troubles are achieving for us an eternal glory that far outweighs them all" (2 Cor 4:17). And when we suffer, as the Apostle Paul says, we are sharing in Christ's "sufferings in order that we may also share in his glory" (Rom 8:17). The Apostle Peter further writes, "Do not be surprised at the painful trial you are suffering, as though something strange were happening to you. But rejoice that you participate in the sufferings of Christ, so that you may be overjoyed when his glory is revealed" (1 Pet 4:12–13). When speaking of suffering, the biblical writers were more often than not referring to actual persecution at the hands of men, but that does not exclude any other sort of suffering from yielding to glory. Begrudgingly, the Apostle Paul boasts of his own sufferings referring to all sorts of trials, from shipwrecks, to hunger, to sleep depravation, and even to the pressures of work (2 Cor 11:22–29). Of one particular hardship of Paul's, Christ said, "My grace is sufficient for you, for my power is made perfect in weakness" (2 Cor 12:9). To which the Apostle Paul responded, "That is why, for Christ's sake, I delight in weaknesses, in insults, in hardships, in persecutions, in difficulties. For when I am weak, then I am strong" (2 Cor 12:10). I said that the Apostle Paul was irksome; I did not lie. Oh how we may wish that we would be transformed by our skills, and our successes and our strength, but that is not the way, it never has been.

It is only through Christ, through his perfection, through his nature, and through his body that we find healing. And healing is an appropriate word, for our sin is like a sickness, and our nature like a grave injury. For such an injury, your strength is not a help, but a hindrance. Like a wounded wild animal we snarl, and beat, and bare our strength, never suspecting that the one approaching comes to help. To be healed, you must submit, must go under the surgeon's knife, must be rendered weak. And in this, you will be made strong. "Though outwardly we are wasting away, yet inwardly we are being renewed day by day" (2 Cor 4:16).

I doubt that this is music to anyone's ears; it is certainly not to mine. There are some things that can, and cannot be done. If pain is to serve any purpose it must remain painful; it cannot be dulled enough to be pleasant, or allayed enough to be dismissed, for to do so would emasculate its very reason for being. But if that was all there was to it, it would be more tolerable. The insult to our injuries is that the good Christian is suppose to *delight* in them. If I must endure suffering, then I must, but why should I have to smile about it, what drivel is that? Shall I taste what is bitter and call it sweet? No, I do not believe that the Christian is called to pretend; whom would you be trying to fool? There is no chance you could fool God, and little chance you could fool yourself. Perhaps that is the real problem with pain; it unmasks all. If I truly wished to be like Christ, if that was my heart's desire, then it would be natural to rejoice in the sufferings that are achieving that goal. What pain illuminates in me is that too often my desire is not directed heavenward, and I secretly do not really wish to be like God. This, then, is the question before us: Do you really want to be like Christ? "Can you drink the cup I drink?" Jesus asks (Mark 10:38).

It is not rejoicing in pain for pain's sake, for Christ prayed, "Father if it is possible, may this cup be taken from me" (Matt 26:39). Rather, it is rejoicing in what God is doing *through* the pain, that God is making us like him. If you do not wish to be like Christ, then there can be no joy in sharing in his sufferings. But how can we make ourselves want to be like Christ? I am not sure that we can, that is in God's power, but we must do what we can. If you cannot summon joy in your sufferings, then summon patience. If you cannot be thankful, be understanding. If you cannot muster praises, silence your complaining. Do the best you can, let God do the rest.

Now there are some very good Christians who recognize that they should rejoice in the Lord through their sufferings, but seem to misunderstand the reason why. I have heard people, after a terrible accident, praise God that their loved ones were only seriously hurt and not more grievously hurt or killed. Although I appreciate the sentiment (God is worthy of praise in all situations), I do not think it is a particularly strong testament to God that things could have been worse. Things can always be worse, and they can also be better. If I am to marvel that God is gracious by only breaking half of my bones, one can retort that it would have been more gracious had he broke none. We are at times missing the point; we are thanking our Father for giving us only three spankings and not four, and not thanking him for the discipline, which is the actual point. Or, if you wish to think of it outside of punishment, it is like an athlete being thankful that the coach is making him run only ten laps instead of twelve, without it ever occurring to him to thank the coach for pushing him to be physically fit, which is the very reason for the laps to begin with. It is good to be thankful for what you have, and natural to realize what you have when tragedies strike, but there is a bigger point than that, and a grander purpose. The glory of the Great Physician is not in sparing you from something worse, but in preparing you for something immeasurably greater.

A lesser cynic might be content to stop here. I think it has been shown justifiable to call God the Great Physician even in light of our enduring physical maladies, for our immortal selves are of greater importance, and God uses our infirmities to heal and grow our everlasting selves in preparation for glorified and perfect bodies. Even so, the voice of the cynic whispers in my own mind an objection. I am not of the mindset that every pain experienced must have deep spiritual significance. When I trip and fall I am more likely to attribute my injuries to my own clumsiness then God's work of refashioning my being. Can't an accident just be an accident, or must we assign divine intention to my ungraceful plummet? Put in those terms it seems rather silly to credit sanctification with every minor cut and bruise, but is it sensible to say that some pain is arbitrary and other pain sacred? Is it not more plausible that all of it is arbitrary and we are just spiritualizing our pain in order to give our suffering meaning? We could certainly come up with numerous reasons for every minor blunder; perhaps God is reminding us to be humble, or reminding us of the great pain Christ endured, or perhaps God is just providing our amusement, after all, a toppling human is at times good for a laugh. But to my ear, such reasons sound hollow.

My argument thus far has been that God does not encase his followers in a protective bubble, because pain is useful and necessary for being healed spiritually, so that in us God might form a particular new creation. However, if we accept that some pain is trivial and neither useful nor necessary for sanctification, then it seems to have no function, which begs the question regarding why it remains.[1] Either every stubbed

---

1. By "trivial" pain, I do not simply mean mild pain. I mean pain that, *prima facie*, does not play a part in our sanctification. Mild pain seems to fit well, but there is some pain experienced that is far from mild, but also uneventful. I hope I am speaking universally, and that you too, have an innate sense for distinguishing between trivial pain and sanctifying pain.

toe plays a part in our regeneration, which on its face seems absurd, or Christ's followers endure some degree of pain for no apparent reason. Perhaps that is a false dichotomy. After all, at times the breaking of bread and drinking of wine is a holy sacrament, and other times, it is just eating.

It is quite clear that our world has a certain nature, a method of operating that is so unrelentingly obeyed that we call it the Law of Nature. In most respects the steadfastness of the Law of Nature is a great blessing. Without it, life would not be possible. There are volumes upon volumes written on the fine-tuning of the universe, indicating that if only one parameter of the universe were just slightly altered, then all known life would be extinct. Beyond the benefit of life (and what a magnificent benefit), the consistency of the laws allows for the better *quality* of life. Because the Law is constant, it is knowable, and because it is knowable, it can be exploited for our good. All of the benefits of medicine and technology are due to the conformity of those laws. And yet, the composition of the ground that makes it a solid foundation on which to build shelters is also what causes me pain when I fall. Whenever I trip, it is possible to imagine that God could intervene and prevent the pain; perhaps God could change the gravity around me so that I fall gently to the ground, or perhaps God could change the composition of the ground that I fall on to be soft like pillows. I am sure we can imagine numerous means for God to prevent my pain, and God many more than we. But he doesn't. And so, if it is indeed trivial pain, we must ask why he doesn't? The laws of nature that govern us provide our first clue.

The laws of nature are like the rules of a game. If the rules of a game were constantly changing, you would never be able to understand the game, and therefore, would never be able to really *play* it. Rules provide the framework for understanding, and the means for playing the game. I do not think that a stubbed toe is meaningful in and of itself, but that it stands as part of a framework that *is* meaningful.

When I was a child I went over to my friend's house, and there in the front yard were two large metallic containers that are commonly used for freight shipping. To my eyes, they stood between ten and twelve feet high, with a space between the two containers of about five feet. It occurred to my friend and me that it might be fun to climb up one of the containers, and jump to the other. I cannot remember exactly how, but we managed to climb to the top. Now these containers, as is common, were not smooth, but had ridges throughout. Because of this, the surface we had to run along had rather deep grooves; and we had to run, for though the gap between the containers was not very great, it did require some momentum to clear. As I stood there preparing to make the jump, a great fear swelled inside me. I imagined my foot snagging on one of those grooves just as I was about to leap, and I pictured myself falling headfirst to the ground. And after I imagined that, I ran, and I jumped.

I doubt very much that any injury I might have incurred by jumping would have been to my spiritual glory. I was up on the container for trivial reasons, and jumping for a silly one; any broken arm or leg that might have resulted, seems to me, would be pain that is nothing but the natural consequence to my frivolity. But if the world we live in were one where God changed the rules for triviality, there would be something very different, and something missing in that event. On that container, I knew the rules of the game; there was no possibility in my mind that God would change the nature of gravity, or the composition of the ground. I knew with absolute certainty that if I fell there would be pain—and then I leapt. It was courageous: silly courage, yes, trivial courage, yes, certainly, but courage nonetheless. Because the laws are constant I had the opportunity to be courageous, even if insignificantly. And by finding courage in times when it does not matter, I will know how to summon it when it does. The first jump was the toughest; the other ones came easy.

The young of the animal world play in order to learn what to do when in more serious situations, and so it is with us. A stubbed toe means nothing in and of itself, but the consistency of the orderly world in which stubbed toes can occur, provides the playground to practice for what really matters. Trivial pain is just that: trivial, not meaningless. It is not of the same importance as the pain that leads to glory; it was the scars from the nails that were a part of Jesus' glorified body, not the blisters he got from walking. The Christian need not regard all pain as equal, it seems silly to do so, but all pain has a reason. It is one thing to be hungry, it is quite another to be starving, but both provide a framework for understanding what Christ meant when he said, "I am the bread of life" (John 6:35). Though hunger pangs at six o'clock and dinner at seven may seem a trivial matter, it can nevertheless put into you the practice of patience, endurance, and perseverance, and I assure you that when you are starving, you will need that. In a strange way, trivial pain exists to make important pain easier, for we have, in some degree, been trained and conditioned for it. I do not mean to make more of trivial pain than it deserves, it is the Lamaze to our childbirth; it cannot remove the need to go through it, and it can seem to us as only a feeble help, but when we are truly sharing in Christ's sufferings, any help is welcomed help.

I do not wish to end a chapter on the Great Physician on such a note, however there is an element of the topic that is intrinsically unsavory. To be in need of a physician is never ideal. To be healed requires an ailment first. It is somewhat surprising then that the idea of God as our physician is so beloved. Shouldn't we prefer an image that does not necessitate our own suffering? And yet, there is nothing that generates more excitement in the believer than a miraculous healing. Perhaps it is not so surprising after all; there are few things that manifest the nature of God so clearly. In one healing touch from God we see his presence, his power, his love, and his caring. But a time is coming when we will not just glimpse his nature, but will be bathed in it, surrounded by God's presence, and engulfed in his love. Miraculous healings serve as a foreshadowing of what is to come. But we must always remember that what is coming is greater. If there is a comforting word for the suffering believer it is this: your prayer for healing will be granted, it is only a question of when. In all the stories that we read of supernatural healing, did you ever wonder how long they endured their suffering before the healing came? Some are described as being afflicted from birth (John 9:1, Acts 3:2). How long they must have endured, how greatly they must have suffered, how terrible their struggle must have been going through life crippled or blind, and forced to beg in order to survive. Until one day, their grief turned to joy when Jesus of Nazareth came to them. Press on, press on, for Christ is coming again, he is coming to heal, and to heal completely, and your grief will turn to joy. "In this world you will have trouble. But take heart! I have overcome the world" (John 16:33). Christ is coming, he has a plan; the Great Physician is coming.

4

God Has A Plan: But You May Not Like It

"'For I know the plans I have for you,' declares the LORD, 'plans to prosper you and not to harm you, plans to give you hope and a future.'" If fine print is to teach us anything, it is that context is important; and there are few verses that are so frequently taken out of context as Jeremiah 29:11. It is never a good idea to only read *a* Bible verse, but it is a particularly bad idea to only read *a* Bible verse that begins with the word "for." "For," at the beginning of a sentence is always used to indicate a continuation of a thought. If you do not know what the preceding thought is, you stand as much chance of interpreting it correctly as accurately following directions that begin with "secondly." It is not surprising that the preceding verse in Jeremiah is so unceremoniously lopped off from devotionals, as well as inspirational calendars or cards, for this is what it says: "When seventy years are completed for Babylon, I will come to you and fulfill my gracious promise to bring you back to this place." Verse ten is certainly less literarily eloquent than its successor, but I doubt that its omission from Christian taglines stems from aesthetics. More likely, it is because it breaks the spell of our self-absorption. "Seventy years? Babylon? What does that have to do with *me*?" we may ask. The enchantment is suddenly dampened as it dawns on us that the "you" referenced is not pertaining (at least not directly) to you or I, and if it is not about us, then the plans for prosperity and hope cited are not directed toward us either.

I am not suggesting that it is wrong to say that God has a benevolent plan for you, for he certainly does. But it is not a matter of simply having the right answer; how you came to that answer is of equal importance. It is one thing to get your sums right because you know how to add, it is another thing entirely to be right because you guessed. You can be right for the wrong reasons. If you apply the word of God out of context you will be lucky to find truth, and taking promises of God that are given to another as your own is the first step to being disappointed with God. We must be cautious not to inject ourselves into descriptive text, mindful not to put promises into the mouth of God that were never uttered to us, and wary not to mistake God's past providence for some as his future plan for us. If there is to be any hope in deciphering what God's plan for us is, we must be certain that the plan actually pertains to *us*. I sincerely believe that God has a good plan for you, a plan not to harm you, a plan of hope and a future, but not because he used those words once to a band of exiles in Babylon.

When speaking of God's plan there is a tendency to shroud it in mystery. In part it is mysterious, but it is also surprisingly straightforward. I have no doubt that there is much unknown, and more to know of what *is* known. There are secret things, for "the secret things belong to the LORD our God," *but* "the things revealed belong to us and to our children forever" (Deut 29:29). There are absolutely secret things, but there are also things revealed, and the one fact does not undo the other. There is much to the physics of gravity that I am ignorant of, but that does not make me shocked when objects fall to the ground. With so much of God already in mystery, it would be a shame to obfuscate what he has made clear. And one of the things God has made clear, one of the things God has revealed to us, is his plan.

We have already heard that "in all things God works for the good of those who love him, who have been called according to his purpose" (Rom 8:28). Moreover, those of us in Christ already know with certitude what is in store for us: that our hope is in Christ, and our future is perfection and glory with him. Everyone who has been instructed in the Truth has received a glimpse into the divine plan. We know that Christ is coming to judge the world so that every wrong will be set right, and we know that those of us who believe in the Son will be resurrected as children of God and coheirs in his glory, to our everlasting joy (Rom 8:16–18). That is God's good plan, plainly spoken to us, and about us. As strange as it may seem on paper, the sad truth is, for most Christians, that plan is of little interest. What is more captivating than the eternal plan of salvation, and by far the most mentally consuming, is God's specific, temporal plan for you or I. Jeremiah 29:11, for example, is more likely conjured as a backdrop to a graduation ceremony than to eternity. But does that not strike you as backward? What plan could be of greater importance than God's eternal one? To place more importance on the here and now, to castigate God for temporal troubles when eternity in fellowship with God is imminent, is a byproduct of a mind unable, or perhaps unwilling, to truly fathom the everlasting. In our better moments, we must sound the amen to the words of an old hymn, that "the things of earth will grow strangely dim, in the light of his glory and grace."[1]

I do not think God's eternal plan can be over emphasized, and any discussion pertaining to God's providence is fundamentally lacking if it is not affirmed. The eternal plan laid out before us, revealed to us in candid terms, must be at the forefront of our thinking. Now having said that, I will, for the moment, let God's eternal plan be; not because it is of less importance, but because it is not where we struggle. It is, of course, only natural to be more intrigued with what is unknown than with what is known. More than that, our fixation on God's temporal plan, rather than God's eternal plan, can come from a very sincere and good desire to remain in line with God's will. With God's eternal plan, we do not perceive a means for us to fall outside of his will, but in our frail state, there is a fear that we will err in our life decisions and fail in our duties to God's sovereign plan. Such fears are misplaced, and wildly inconsistent. Misplaced, because to fear dissonance with God's will demonstrates a heart that seeks his will. Inconsistent, because we fret our accordance with God's will in only some, but not all decisions. For instance, when you put on clothes this morning, did you worry whether the outfit you chose was in accordance with God's plan for you? I suspect not; but if not, why not? Is there really so great a difference between choosing a career and choosing a jacket? The former will certainly impact your life to a greater degree, but they are alike, in that they are moral equals. And that is really the point; to be outside of God's desired will is to be in sin. To choose something contrary to God's desired will, is to deliberately, and willfully, disobey God. It is never simply an honest mistake. The idea that we who seek God's guidance will miss his answer and accidentally stray off the path because God's voice was too soft and too small, or our ears too untrained, does not have the support of either reason or Scripture. It is unreasonable to believe that an omnipotent God somehow needs help in communicating with his own subjects. If God wishes to speak to you, he will. There is no prerequisite for hearing God, there is only obedience or disobedience when he speaks. That is our choice;

1. "Turn Your Eyes Upon Jesus," words and music by Helen H. Lemmel.

there is no reason to think we can plead ignorance, and no scriptural evidence to support such a notion. Eve knew what God's will was when she took of the forbidden fruit, Moses knew what God's will was when he struck the rock, the Israelites knew what God's will was when they refused to conquer the land he had given them, Jonah knew what God's will was when he fled, and the list goes on. If God has told you to be of a certain vocation, or move to a certain place, or marry a certain person, then do so, and if he has told you to wear red socks, do that as well.

We must of course be diligent to not mistake our own voice for God. Not because God's voice is too faint and ours to brash, and certainly not because his voice sounds like ours, but rather, because our voice is the most pleasing to our own ears. There is one idol with a mouth that speaks, and he is the worst of them all.

It is interesting to note that God's plan prophesied in Jeremiah 29 is given in sharp contrast to the prophesies of men. "Do not let the prophets and diviners among you deceive you," God says. "Do not listen to the dreams *you* encourage them to have. They are prophesying lies to you in my name" (Jer 29:8–9; emphasis mine). God's good plan was not to their satisfaction so, instead of obedience, many turned to their own purposes and followed their own voices. To those who disobeyed and refused to go into exile, God said, "I will pursue them with the sword, famine and plague and will make them abhorrent to all the kingdoms of the earth and an object of cursing and horror, of scorn and reproach, among all the nations where I drive them. For they have not listened to my words . . . words that I sent to them again and again by my servants the prophets" (Jer 29:18–19). It was not in ignorance that they refused to obey God, for he spoke to them *again*, and *again*. There was not a shroud of mystery in it, no plausible deniability, no simple miscommunication. There was obedience or disobedience; there was serving God or serving self.

I do not think that the folly of the Israelites is unique to them. We too disregard God's plan when it differs from our wisdom. It is certainly true the sheep of the Good Shepherd know his voice, but that does not mean they will like it. Because we *should* be gratified by God's voice, we think, *ipso facto*, that we will. But that is the difference between what is and what should be, and that is a very great difference indeed. It seems though, that the bigger problem is not the difference between is and ought, but between what seems good to God and what seems good to us.

Amidst struggles and difficult circumstances, the good is at times hard to see; what is evil can be mistaken for good, and what is good, mistaken for evil. Light can be as blinding as engulfing darkness, but that does not mean they are the same thing.

How then, are we to understand God's plan as good, when all other paths seem better, and all other plans seem finer? What, after all, is good about being captive in Babylon for seventy years? Not much in and of itself, but is that the whole story? If we judge God's plan by only one of its parts we make a very grave error. To say that a good plan must be free of bad parts is as silly as saying a good book must be free of bad events. Murder, rape, betrayal, and lies, though objectively bad, may be a part of any good book; in fact, such things can *contribute* to what makes the book good. In some of the same way God takes what is bad in isolation, and transforms it to be good in whole. Even the greatest single event in all of human history, if examined only in isolation, would be regarded with nothing but scorn. Without the broader context, the Passion is nothing short of abhorrent. There is no better example of God's remarkable ability to transform what is horrid to what is holy than the cross, the "eucatastrophe," as dubbed by Tolkien. That is our Lord's *modus operandi*; he takes what is bad and makes it good, he takes the wretch and makes him a son, he takes the shame of a crucifixion and makes it his glory.

The Israelites regarded seventy years of exile as bad, and of course it was, but in a broader context it was good, for it was good for God to punish a people that had forsaken him. And it was good for another reason too. Listen to what God says about seventy years of captivity: "Then you will call upon me and come and pray to me, and I will listen to you. You will seek me and find me when you seek me with all your heart" (Jer 29:12–13). It is certainly not good to be in exile, but it is better to be in exile and seeking God than to be in your own kingdom without desire for him. At times God's plan may not seem good to us; it may even contain elements that we correctly label as *bad*. But we must remember that God is a God of transformation, and it is not unusual in Christian lives to have our greatest hardships become the source of our greatest blessings. Should we expect any different from a God whose chosen people were fathered by a man with a barren wife? On the road to Damascus the Apostle Paul was struck blind, a terrible event in itself, but I do not think Paul would disagree with me if I said that it was the greatest thing that ever happened to him. If the world around us seems utterly dark, we might very well be blind, but we might have been blinded with light.

My contention is simple: that God works out all things for the good of those who love him, who have been called according to his purpose, and that his purpose for you is good, whether it looks like it or not, or whether you like it or not. But perhaps this misses the real issue. It could be said that our grievances are not against God's plan, but against his silence. We might very well approve of God's plan and praise him for it, if only we were let in the loop! The Israelites were given fair warning: they were provided reason for their captivity, told of its duration, and foretold of its outcome; but God is not so forthcoming for me, and I suspect, for you. God certainly *speaks* to me, the Holy Spirit teaches me, convicts me, prompts me to worship, and in that way speaks to me. But there is rarely an instance, (I can think of only one) in which the speech is what we would call prophetic. God does not, but for the rarest of occasions, let me in on the plan. Prophecy is labeled as a spiritual gift, and like all spiritual gifts, not everyone has it (Rom 12:6).[2] This can be a source of great frustration. For we feel that we could take on any hardship, face any challenge, persevere through any suffering, if only we knew the outcome, and the reason for it. As much as we may feel that way, it simply is not true; for we already know what the outcome is, and what the reason is. God has told us that the outcome is good, and the reason for our hardships, our challenges, our sufferings, is that they are good for us, and good for others.

But that is too generic! What we want are specifics. *How* is God going to make this good? *How* exactly will this be good for me? I am sympathetic to these questions, and will try my best to answer them in some manner, but I think we must first acknowledge the source of these questions. We have heard, and I will say it again, that God works out all things for the good of those who love him, who have been called according to his purpose, for that is what God has told us in his word. But it seems that we do not believe God. If we truly believed God, we would not need the details, for the demands for the minutia with God are only ever motivated by distrust. Our sensory experience, when at odds with

---

2. It should be noted that prophecy is a gift that must be used with care. It is a very dangerous thing to claim to speak the words of God; false prophets of the past came to very bad fates. Any prophecy given must be in harmony with God's inspired word, and any who have gifts of prophecy must be carefully scrutinized and tested as the prophets of old were.

God, leads us to doubt him. But this I think is a mistake, not because our senses are unreliable, but because they are limited. Our senses cannot tell us what is to come, and what is to come may transfigure our present. I do not mean to stifle good questions, and I have no desire to advocate blind, unjustified faith. I merely wish to hold some measure of scrutiny over ourselves, and direct a few questions our way, for I am certain that with scrutiny God will be justified, and our distrust unjustified. Is it really more logical to rely on our own, limited faculty in the face of omniscience? Is there anything in our experience of God that leads us to distrust him? Do we have any evidence, any at all, to make the case that God is suspect or mendacious? If we can level no charge against God, then why do we continue to lack faith? If God is who he says he is, where is our knowledge of him deficient? At some point, we must question whether we really believe this business of Christianity or not. If your logic convinces, if your experience validates, and if your heart confirms its truth, then believe with confidence, and if not, then do not. But let us do our very best to stop straddling belief, to stop saying with one breath that God works out all things for good, and in the next ponder if that really applies in *this* particular instance.

I think now we are ready to return to our initial question: Why is God not more forthcoming with the details of his plan? To begin, I am not convinced that details will help us as much as we would think. Is there really so great a comfort in having a detailed roadmap leading to a place you do not want to go? Certain knowledge is comforting, but some only troubles the mind. I have heard many Christians, when reflecting on their walk with God, express that they would never have done x if they had known z. I believe that God gives us the knowledge that will aid us most. I must then conclude, that it is not the details that we need most.

I confess I do not know the answers to the questions of your hardships. I am not privy to the specifics of how God will work out his goodness, I do not know the details, for "who has known the mind of the Lord? Or who has been his counselor?" (Rom 11:34). I simply do not know what God's specific temporal plan for me is, much less his plan for you. But this I do know: I know God. And this is knowledge that aids me better.

In reading through the Old Testament, God's previous method of communication might strike the modern Christian as being utterly foreign. In comparison to our modern times, would it not be at moments preferable to have a godly man, verified and tested to speak on behalf of God, boldly proclaim in plain terms what the Lord exactly sayeth? I am not denying that God does on occasion speak to us in ways of old, but it is, if nothing else, less common. A fundamental change has occurred. The author of Hebrews writes, "In the past God spoke to our forefathers through the prophets at many times and in various ways, but in these last days he has spoken to us by his Son" (Heb 1:1–2). As much as we may not realize it, as much as it may not seem like it at times, the communication of the Son is superior to that of the prophets, for, "the Son is the radiance of God's glory and the exact representation of his being" (Heb 1:3). To God's people of old, he gave greater details of his temporal plan, but to us, God gives the greater details of who he is. This is not done arbitrarily, for before Christ, God dealt with and related with his people in old creation terms. In those days, an afterlife was debatable and uncertain at best, and all blessings, promises, and punishments of God were given in concrete worldly ways, such as blessings of peace and prosperity, health, and longevity of life, land and food aplenty. And the punishments consisted of war, famine, enslavement, disease, and death. Even that which we would call *spiritual* was manifested in earthly physical terms, with a temple, an ark, and animal sacrifice. In light of Christ, all of these things have taken on new meaning, but more than that, with Christ we have been given real knowledge of eternity, of spiritual blessing, and of new life.

Jesus ushered in the beginning of the new creation. The old way is passing and a new order is rising in its place. What is to replace the old is so drastically different, so radically new that it is very difficult for us to understand, and I suspect in some ways, impossible to. To combat this, God has given images and pictures to help us, but those are just shadows for a mind unable to fully comprehend. This, I think, is the reason why God does not speak to us in the same way as in the past. God's plan is for the new creation, and there are no words in the old order that truly captures the new. It is like trying to explain color to a man born blind. We do not, as remnants of the old creation, have the faculty to decipher the new. If this is true, then even if God were to give us a detailed roadmap of his plan, it would, at least in part, be unintelligible to us. God could speak to the Israelites in plain concrete terms because he was dealing with the old creation, a medium that man is fully immersed in and thus comprehendible. But with one foot in the old creation and the other in the new, we are at a loss. We are the flatlanders who have heard and believe in another dimension, but who cannot fathom how a square becomes a cube. And so, if you cannot decipher the roadmap, you must rely on your guide.

Knowing our inability, God increases our knowledge of him, so that we may trust his guidance. I may not receive the prophetic declaration of God's plan, but daily he tells me who he is through his word, through the example of his Son, and the teaching, and moving of the Holy Spirit in my life and the lives of my fellow brothers and sisters. This is done so that what we cannot know (and there is much about the new creation that we cannot) is overcome by faith in what we do know, namely Jesus.

At this point we might be tempted to think better of ourselves and less of God than is probably warranted. We might think that we are in fact capable of understanding God's plan, and even if we couldn't, what is the harm in taking a whack at it? Furthermore, shouldn't omnipotence, no matter how complex the concept, be able to communicate effectively? Didn't we say that it was unreasonable otherwise? To the first objection, omniscience knows quite well what we are capable of, and if we are in fact incapable, I cannot hold it against God to omit something that does not benefit us at all. To the second objection, I think we must clarify what omnipotence really means. Omnipotence is not the ability to do *anything*; it is the ability to do anything that is *possible*. There are certain things that God cannot do. For one, God cannot sin. God cannot do what is logically contradictory, like make square circles. It may be a bit troubling for some to say that God cannot do something, but follow the reason why. It is not that God cannot make square circles because God lacks the power (which is what omnipotence is really referring to), God cannot make square circles because the idea of a square circle is nonsensical. Logical incoherence does not undermine God's power.

If God cannot communicate to us how exactly our current circumstances are fulfilling his plan for the new creation, it must be because it is logically contradictory to do so. This is not as confusing as it may seem. Even in our own lives, there are some things that cannot truly be explained, they can only be experienced. How does one explain the color green to a man born blind? I could describe things that are green, I could talk about light and tell him that green is light with a spectrum wavelength of 520 to 570 nanometers, and though accurate, that brings him no closer to understanding what green really is. Real knowledge and understanding of green is gained only experientially. And so it may be with the new creation: it may be a thing that cannot be explained, only experienced in order to be truly understood. And we must, therefore, have the necessary faculty in order *to* experience it, just as we must have eyes to really understand color. As it stands, we do not have the faculty to experience the new creation. You may argue that God could give us the faculty to understand it, just as he could give sight to a blind man in order for him to experience color. I completely agree with that, and in fact, that is what God is going to do. Those of us in Christ will be transformed, and will possess the faculty to experience the new creation, and thereby understand it. But there is a subtle distinction here. Squares cannot be circles because they have contradictory attributes, so you cannot have a square circle; but that is not to say that a square cannot be transformed *into* a circle. When the old order has passed away the new may come, when a square ceases to be a square it may become a circle. We are going to be resurrected as new creations and will undergo a radical transformation that is far more dramatic than even a change from square to circle. But until we are *fully* transformed into those dynamically new creatures we will not have the faculty to understand the new creation.

To summarize, there are some things about God's plan that cannot be explained to us because they pertain to the new creation, and we do not possess the faculty to experience, and hence understand the new creation. We will gain the ability to understand the new creation only when we are resurrected as wholly new beings into the new creation. Squares may become circles, but you cannot have square circles.

Some may object that I am stipulating that we will *become* new creations, when it clearly says in 2 Corinthians: "if anyone is in Christ, he is a new creation; the old has gone, the new has come!" (2 Cor 5:17). And if we are already new creations, then of course we must have the faculty to experience the new creation and therefore understand God's plan. So why does God not reveal it? Well, I think this misconstrues the Apostle Paul's words. He uses present tense, but I think he is speaking from an eternal perspective, where past and present tense have no meaning. This is in fact indicated in the preceding verse where he says, "from now on we *regard* no one from a worldly point of view" (2 Cor 5:6; emphasis mine). Paul is *regarding* us as new creations; he is viewing those in Christ from an eternal perspective. Earlier in the chapter he states, "while we are in this tent, we groan and are burdened, because we do not wish to be unclothed but to be clothed with our heavenly dwelling, so that what is mortal may be swallowed up by life" (2 Cor 5:4). You do not groan for what you already have; if we are already new creations there should be no need for longing.

Now, I am not suggesting that the process of sanctification is not taking place, or that we are not at present being actively transformed into new creations. But I think that can only be taken so far. As long as we have one foot in the old world we can never fully experience the new. There is a line that must be crossed. For most, that line will be death, where you may finally rid yourself completely of the old creation, and be fully born again to experience the new. If you do not mind being somewhat ridiculous, I have an example that might help illustrate what I mean. Let us pretend that the new man will be an aquatic being. We at present are obviously land creatures, and not naturally suited to live an aquatic life. However, we could still, though land creatures, learn and study about water, we could live on a houseboat, we could learn to swim, and snorkel for hours and scuba dive, we could put goggles on our eyes to help us see underwater, and flippers on our feet to help us move in water, and in that way we could become *more* aquatic than we would otherwise be. But that can only be taken so far; at some point our physiology prevents us from being true aquatic beings. I think sanctification is much the same way: there are many things we can do, or can be done to us, to prepare us and develop us to become more like the new creation, but at some point the old creation prevents us from being true new creations. There is a barrier that must be overcome, but we may rest assured that it will be, for the Holy Spirit is said to be "a deposit, guaranteeing what is to come" (2 Cor 5:5).

We may wish that the complete transformation into new creations would come sooner rather than later, and that is a fine thing to wish, but God knows the right time; it is all part of his plan. In the meantime, God has something in mind for you. I have spent most of this chapter talking about what God is going to do in his plan, and very little discussing our roles in his plan. So here it is: God's temporal plan for you is that at all times, in every circumstance and life situation you find yourself in, be Christ's ambassador, witnessing and teaching to all about Jesus Christ, by obeying God's commands and loving him with all your heart and with all your soul and with all your mind, and loving your neighbor as yourself. This has been told to us from the beginning, there is no great mystery in it, and not much more that can be said.

5

Faith Is A Virtue: But Not All Faith

WE HAVE, TILL THIS point, been examining more closely the Christian tenets of God's attributes, like God's love, justness, and sovereignty. I hope that the discussion thus far has been helpful, and that by scrutinizing our beliefs about God we are developing a more robust theology. But at this point I wish to address the fine print of a belief that is not about God, but about Christians.

As we have seen, the Christian defines what is good based on God, for God *is* good. Our good attributes are but mimicry of God: we are told to love because God is the manifestation of the qualities of love; we are told to be just because God is just; we are told to be righteous because God is righteous, and so on. But one of the most cherished attributes of a good Christian is, as it turns out, not an attribute that God possesses, and that is faith. God does not have faith, for his omniscience precludes it. A necessary condition of faith is a deficiency of knowledge, but God knows everything, and so he has no need of faith. Faith is necessary for us because, as we saw in the last chapter, there are things that we cannot know, there are elements of God's nature that are, as the theologians say, incommunicable to us. This side of eternity God's incommunicable attributes, his infinitude, his omniscience, his omnipresence, and the like, will never be fully knowable. Indeed, even in the everlasting, we may still stand in amazement and awe as we increasingly gain knowledge of God, but, perhaps, never exhaust all knowledge of him.

Since faith is not an inherent part of God's nature it cannot be inherently good, as other attributes of God are good. Righteousness and justness, for instance, are attributes of God that are inherent to him and so inherently good. And because righteousness and justness are inherently good they cannot be misapplied, for to misapply them is to not practice them. You cannot sin by being truly righteous, and you cannot sin by being truly just, but you can most certainly sin by being truly faithful. For faith is not an inherently good thing, it is only good with qualification. There is nothing virtuous about a devout Muslim faithfully serving a false god by killing himself in order to kill others so that he may gain entrance to Heaven and be rewarded with numerous virgins and rivers of wine. Such a man is certainly a man of incredible faith, who follows through with his belief even unto death. But that is not to be admired, nor will it be credited to him as righteousness, because faith is not inherently virtuous. Faith for faith's sake is not enough. You have to be right. How is it to your credit to have faith in something that is unworthy of it? That is why it is important to know why you believe what you believe. Sound logical reasoning, good theology, the reading of the Scriptures, and the fellowship of the body of believers are all important, because all of those things confirm, and reinforce and give reason for our beliefs, and that strengthens and encourages our faith. To indiscriminately ascribe faith as virtuous is a mistake too often committed, and has led to some embarrassing misunderstandings in the culture about what faith is.

There are many in our culture who regard the modern Christian as a superstitious simpleton. One who rejects reason in favor of religious fervor, and clings to faith while the rest of the world stands assuredly on facts. And this charge against the Christian intellect is based, not on any form of standardized test, IQ statistic, or academic background, but on the unwavering esteemed importance the Christian has placed on faith. It should not surprise us that faith is so off-putting to the irreligious, when faith has been incorrectly described as "belief that does not rest on logical proof or material evidence." Others have defined faith as "warrantless or baseless belief," and some have even gone so far as to claim that faith is, "belief that is contrary to evidence." Our culture has accepted these definitions of faith and under them has mocked religious faith, or worse has patronizingly portrayed baseless belief as somehow being noble. And the Christian has been slow to correct them.

In fact, I believe Christians have unintentionally championed these bogus ideas of faith by emphasizing a distinction between "people of faith" and "people of no faith." How often have we heard the proud proclamation of, "I am a person of faith"? We wear it like a badge of honor. But as we have seen, faith is not inherently good, and so to boast that you are a person of faith is either a silly sentence or an incomplete one.

The simple truth is, every man, whether they admit it or not, is a man of faith. It is unavoidable.

If the world is to dislike us (and they will), let them at least dislike us for the right reasons, and not because we have improperly defined a central component of our religion. To correct this, let us start with a more fitting definition of faith. Simply put, faith is the follow through of belief. Some have considered faith and belief to be synonymous, but there is a subtle difference. After all, they cannot be exactly the same thing, as it is possible to have belief without faith. There are people who believe (with good reason) that planes can take off, fly, and land safely—but they will never step foot on one. They have belief, but not faith. Or, we Christians might believe (with good reason) that God is sovereign and that God is in control, yet our lives are full of worry and anxiety. We have belief, but not faith. This is what I think the Apostle James is referring to when he says faith without deeds is not really faith at all, for belief is passive, but faith is active (Jas 2:14).

Now, everyone has beliefs and everyone puts their faith into those beliefs. You might believe that a friend is trustworthy, so in faith, you tell them your secrets. You might believe that a rollercoaster is safe, so in faith you get on one. You might believe that anesthesia works, so in faith you will go under the surgical knife.

Faith is a universal experience. Those same people who mock so-called "people of faith" are themselves living by faith every time they board a plane or share something in confidence. These same people would never regard their actions as illogical, irrational, or stupid and yet they regard faith as inherently illogical, irrational, and stupid. That is why I feel the "people of faith," or "person of faith" terminology is harmful, because it does not make the right distinction. The distinction between the Christian and the non-Christian is not that we have faith and they do not, but that we have faith in Christ. And that is where the distinction *should* be made.

If we continue to advocate that religious people are the only people of faith, we grossly misrepresent faith, and allow the atheist to claim they have no faith. And if they are free from faith, then they are free to smear *all* faith as irrational. But if faith is the follow-through of belief, then whether it is rational or not depends entirely on what it is you believe. If our belief is irrational, our faith will be irrational, but if our belief is rational then our faith will also be rational. Faith is not inherently good, nor is it inherently irrational. In fact, at times the very *absence* of faith can be *irrational*. Our first example of faith is a good one. The person who refuses to get on a plane due to fear is suffering from a phobia, which by definition is *irrational*. Such lack of faith in air travel is *unreasonable*. This is very important because there are many who wish to bash Christian faith by moving the bar as to what counts as *reasonable* faith. They argue that because we cannot prove God's existence, it is unreasonable to have faith in God. It is certainly true that we cannot prove God (in the very technical sense) for God is not a being that can be subject to testing. But look back at our example; you cannot *prove* to the one with the phobia that his plane will arrive at his destination safely. That is a future event and future events cannot be tested and so cannot be proven. Does that then mean that the one with the phobia holds the rational position because their doubt cannot be proven false? Of course not! The question is not whether or not your faith can be proven, but whether or not your position is reasonable given the evidence.

The Christian is not called to irrational faith, and our belief in God and in his Son is not unreasonable. There is ample evidence to justify reasonable faith in God, and the Christian God in particular. There is scientific evidence formulated well in the cosmological argument, and the teleological argument for the existence of God. There are philosophical reasons for belief, like the argument from morality, or from consciousness. There is historical evidence for the person of Jesus, evidence for his death and resurrection, and evidence of his Godhood. If you are unfamiliar with these arguments, and the evidence that supports them, I encourage you to look into them and to study them.[1] Lastly, there is of course, empirical evidence, such as your personal experience with God and your observation of his transformational working in your life, and the similar testimony of others.

Unfortunately, there are some Christians who do not desire reasons for their faith because they somehow believe blind faith is the only sort of virtuous faith. They believe that to invoke reason and logic is an act of defiance against God, and a demonstration of a lack of faith in him. After all, Jesus said, "Because you have seen me, you have believed, blessed are

---

1. There are many good books on these subjects, but for an introduction to these concepts I would recommend, *Why I Am A Christian*, as it will introduce you to a vast array of arguments for the Christian faith, from multiple Christian authors in the top of their fields.

those who have not seen and still believe" (John 20:29). Furthermore, Jesus also said, "A wicked and adulterous generation asks for a miraculous sign" (Matt 12:39). Don't we deride and look down upon *doubting* Thomas for his demand to see evidence of the resurrected Jesus? Is the Bible then saying that we should not seek evidence for belief but should simply blindly believe in faith?

    I think that this is a misreading of the passages. An illustration might best explain what I think the Scriptures are really pointing to. Imagine a marriage several years underway in which the wife, with no evidence or reason to suspect infidelity, everyday grills her husband with accusing questions, and every week demands he take an STD test, and constantly snoops through his pockets, emails, and voicemails for evidence of adultery. What sort of marriage would you call that? Or suppose that a close friend or relative wants you to watch their kids while they are away, but demand that you undergo a thorough background check beforehand. How would you respond to such a demand? I think you would be a little bit puzzled and probably a bit exasperated. "You know me," you might exclaim. I don't think that it is wrong, or unwarranted for a wife to have evidence for faith in her spouse, or a close friend or relative to have good reason to trust you with the care of their children. But the constant demand for more evidence, and the inability to rest in the knowledge already possessed can become a perversion, just as the illustration demonstrates with the perversion of marriage and of the friendship. This is what I believe the Bible is speaking out against. It is not advocating ignorance, it is not suggesting that you shouldn't have evidence; the issue is of *sufficiency*.

    Doubting Thomas may serve as our good example. Here was a man who spent time with Jesus, who walked with Jesus and ate with Jesus, who heard his powerful teaching and saw Jesus perform numerous miracles with his own eyes. He saw Jesus raise people from the dead. He heard Jesus predict his betrayal, death, burial, and, resurrection. Then after all of that, his close friends, whom he knew were trustworthy, came to him and said, "We have seen the Lord" (John 20:25). And after all of that his response was still disbelief, and disbelief that would not be cured by even his own sight, but had to be enforced by his touch. It is the sufficiency of the evidence already before Thomas that makes his response worthy of derision, not the simple request for evidence.

The idea that blind faith is somehow virtuous is a thought that renders all believers fools. Faith is indeed *necessary* because we cannot know everything, but it is only *useful* because we can know some things. Knowledge is in fact foundational to belief and faith. Faith does not exist in a vacuum, as the Scripture says, "Faith comes from hearing the message, and the message is heard through the word of Christ" (Rom 10:17). A little before in the same chapter it says, "'Everyone who calls on the name of the Lord will be saved.' How, then, can they call on the one they have not believed in? And how can they believe in the one of whom they have not heard? And how can they hear without someone preaching to them?" (Rom 10:13-14). Our faith is not based on what is unknown; it is based and can only ever be based on what *is* known. And what is known is sufficient for faith.

Now the reason God seems to care so much about the sufficiency of faith is because what is sufficient for faith in God is proportionate to relationship. The closer you are to someone, the better the relationship, the more faith you will have in them, and the less evidence you will require of them. It is interesting that Jesus uses the term "adulterous" to describe those who demand from him evidence of his power and authority (Matt 12:38-39). To Jesus, their lack of faith was a manifestation of the damage and brokenness of the relationship. Jesus said, "You do not know me or my Father . . . if you knew me, you would know my Father also" (John 8:20). They should have known Jesus because they should have known his Father, for his Father revealed himself to them, but they strayed from him. That is why Jesus calls them wicked and adulterous. It is not that Jesus was against providing evidence for his power and authority, for he routinely did so. Jesus said, "I have shown you many great miracles from the Father" (John 10:32), and "the miracles I do in my Father's name speak for me" (John 10:25). Jesus further said, "Do not believe me unless I do what my Father does. But if I do it, even though you do not believe me, believe the miracles, that you may know and understand that the Father is in me, and I in the Father" (John 10:37-38). The issue is not of evidence but of sufficiency, and that is never more clearly demonstrated than in the story of the rich man and Lazarus, where Jesus, in the mouth of Abraham declares these words: "If they do not listen to Moses and the Prophets, they will not be convinced even if someone rises from the dead" (Luke 16:31). God wants us to have sufficient evidence and reason for our faith in him, and that is best achieved not with signs and wonders, but with real knowledge of God gained in relationship.

The reason I say knowledge gained in relationship is because there seems to be a distinction between knowledge acquired by mere facts, and knowledge that is acquired through experience. This is sometimes labeled as the difference between head knowledge and heart knowledge, but that is an unfortunate misnomer, for it creates the wrong impression that heart knowledge has no basis in evidence or reason. But of course all knowledge must be based in evidence and reason for that is what makes knowledge *knowable*. The real difference is in the sort of reason and kind of evidence, and that is best explained by analogy.

If you were to skydive for the first time, you could fill your head with all kinds of facts in preparation for the jump. You could learn all there is to know about the physics of skydiving, you could study in detail the history of skydiving, you could theoretically review every anecdote, every testimony, every paper ever written on the subject, and you could know more information about skydiving than even a professional skydiver. And yet, when the airplane doors open, whose knees are more likely to wobble? Who is more likely to have faith in skydiving? It seems that mere facts absent experience are less sufficient for faith. The professional skydiver has knowledge that you do not. He knows what it is like to skydive. He has experiential knowledge.

The knowledge gained in relationship is of course experiential in nature. This is why in our language we make the distinction between knowing *of* someone and knowing someone. To say that you know someone implies a relationship. It implies that you know more than just the facts about someone, but that you have *experienced* someone. God wants us to have more experiential knowledge of him because, as our skydiving illustration shows, experiential knowledge is more conducive for faith than mere facts. This is all very pragmatic. The reason for the importance of sufficiency and faith is very practical.

I once spoke with an atheist who was ridiculing the Christian mantra that "God works in mysterious ways" and characterizing it as nothing more than an intellectual dodge of tough questions. Now it certainly is true that such catchphrases are sometimes invoked as an evasion tactic, however, the underlining principle of the mantra is sound logic. For it is impossible for a finite, temporal, limited mind, such as ours, to understand everything that there is to know about an infinite, eternal being, such as God. That is not a possibility. And to say otherwise, is illogical. As we have said, "The secret things belong to the Lord our God, the things revealed belong to us and to our children forever" (Deut 29:29). There are secret things; there are things about God that you are not going to understand completely. It is not possible for you to acquire all of the facts pertaining to God, and even if you could, much of it would be unintelligible. All created beings are epistemologically handicapped, because our ability to know anything is contingent on something else. I can have no knowledge without senses, and I can have no senses without matter, and there is no matter without creation, and there is no creation without Creator. We are not autonomous in knowledge; we are bound to the epistemological tools that we have been given, and we have no means of testing the reliability of those tools. As J. B. S. Haldane said, "If my mental processes are determined wholly by the motions of atoms in my brain, I have no reason to suppose that my beliefs are true. They may be sound chemically, but that does not make them sound logically. And hence I have no reason for supposing my brain to be composed of atoms."[2] We can only really trust our knowledge by first trusting that God gave us the ability to know. God emphasizes faith in himself because without that as the foundation, faith in anything is ultimately unjustified.

In less metaphysical terms we also find deficiency in our knowledge. As we discussed in the last chapter, much of what God will do falls outside of the realm of our knowledge. We must therefore rely on our knowledge of God, just as we would in any other relationship where our knowledge instruments are futile. If you were to disclose something sensitive to a friend, you could not know with certainty that the friend would honor your confidence. There is no means to know such a thing; we simply have no epistemological tools for it. It cannot be known through scientific testing, nor can it be known through logical deduction. Though we cannot know with certainty what a friend may do in the future, we can, nevertheless have real knowledge of the friend. It is that type of knowledge that leads to faith. We often speak well of childlike faith, and I think that is because young children believe and accept, in faith, what their parents tell them is true, simply because their parents are the ones who said it. A child does not possess great knowledge of the world, for their knowledge instruments are underdeveloped, but a child *does* have knowledge of the parent, and recognizes the authority of the

2. Haldane, *Possible worlds*, 220.

parent, and knows the trustworthiness of the parent, and that is enough for a child's faith. That is sufficient. Their lack of knowledge of the world is overcome by their knowledge of the parent and they are able to respond in faith. As we grow older, we begin to see the fallen-ness of our parents and the fallen-ness of the world, and our faith in them weakens, which is certainly wise. But the problem is we begin to regard God in the same way, as if God is fallen, and that is not wise, logical, or faithful.

The great heroes of faith in the Bible always based their faith on who God is. In the book of Daniel, when Shadrach, Meshach, and Abednego were told to worship the image of gold or be thrown into the fiery furnace, they replied to the king, "O Nebuchadnezzar, we do not need to defend ourselves before you in this matter. If we are thrown into the blazing furnace, the God we serve is able to save us from it, and he will rescue us from your hand, O king. *But even if he does not*, we want you to know, O king, that we will not serve your gods or worship the image of gold you have set up" (Dan 3:16–18; emphasis mine). The most remarkable thing about this passage is not that they had faith that God would save them, but that they had faith even if he would not save them. For their faith was not based on what God would do, it was based on who God is. We would do well to etch this account into our hearts and minds, for it so perfectly encompasses the nature of faith. It demonstrates the necessity of faith due to the deficiency of human knowledge, for they did not know what God would do, or what would happen. At the same time it shows that the knowledge they possessed about God was sufficient for them. What God revealed to them about himself was sufficient for them, and it is sufficient for us as well. It is sufficient for reason, it is sufficient for logic, it is sufficient for belief, and subsequently it is sufficient for faith.

We tend to make the mistake of basing our faith on what God will do, but as we have seen, faith is necessary because there are things we cannot know, but it is not *based* on what we do not know, it is based on what we do know. And what we know is God, what we do not know is what God will do. You might object that we *can* know what God will do, because God has given us promises. You would be right. But what good are God's promises if he is a liar or a cheat? Faith in what God will do presupposes faith in who he is. Do not put the cart before the horse. I would also caution that, although God has given us promises, the fulfillment of them might be nothing like what you would expect.

After all, people who knew of Christ's promises crucified him. I would say it is better to simply have faith in who God is, or you will run the risk of losing faith by expecting God's promises fulfilled in *your* way, and in *your* timing.

One of the most horrendous stories in the word of God concerns Abraham and Isaac. We in the fold of Christendom know the story so well we may at times gloss over it. I find myself oddly grateful to the enemies of our faith for their constant shrieking about the cruelty and malevolence of the Abraham account. Though I think they speak from ignorance, they in a way do it more justice than I, for in my many readings I tend to lull it to mythology, but they speak of it as history, as real events with real people, and real psychology. That is of course exactly how one should read it. Unlike us, Abraham did not know what would happen, he did not know how God would fulfill his promise to him. Abraham did not know that his hand would be stopped, or that he would be spared the loss of his son (Gen 22:1–14). In light of so much uncertainty how is it that Abraham was willing to obey God's command to slay, with his own hand, the fulfillment of God's promise to him? He was willing because of what he knew: he knew God. He had faith in God because he knew God to be faithful. He had trust in God because he knew God to be trustworthy.

We have seen that faith is neither inherently good nor inherently illogical, but is simply the follow-through of belief, which is necessary because of shortcomings in our knowledge, but is grounded in what we do know. What we know is God, sufficiently revealed to us by himself through general revelation, special revelation, and personal relationship with him. That is what faith in God is, but that does not exactly tell us why faith in God is virtuous.

The idea of faith being credited as righteousness is an oddity very rarely pondered in some Christian groups and quite nearly denied in others. For some, the mystery of saving faith is so great that they patch its perceived weakness by works. For the irreligious this is a great difficulty as well, for they cannot understand how it is that they are to perish simply because they do not believe. Is unbelief really so great an offense? Does it not seem that simple belief is an arbitrary barometer for entrance into Heaven? How can it be that all of salvation hinges on our belief in Jesus? To be sure, I do not believe that anyone is punished for unbelief per se. They are punished for sin, but a consequence of sin is that it hinders belief. It is very rare for anyone to reject belief in Christ for intellectual reasons; God is far more commonly rejected because a sinner does not wish to yield his lifestyle to the Lord. As to the issue of faith or deeds, they are really one and the same, for faith is a deed, faith is belief enacted. What saves a man is the belief that Jesus paid for his sins, and the enacting of that belief through repentance, profession, and acceptance of Jesus as his Lord.

I think the mystery of saving faith is aggravated by thinking that it is faith *that* saves. It is not faith that saves; it is God that saves *through* faith. If you and a few others were trapped in a burning building and your only chance for survival was to jump to a fireman's net down below, those who trusted in the fire net and jumped would be saved, and those who did not would perish. But it is the fireman's net that saves you, for if the net could not save you, your faith in it most certainly could not. We are not saved by faith; we are saved by God through faith, just as we are saved by the fireman's net through our faith in it. The net can save you, only if you step out in faith and jump, and in the same way, Jesus saves only by putting your faith in Christ and inviting him in as Lord. I suppose it is theoretically possible that God could have brought salvation to men by a different means. But for whatever reason, God has chosen this way, and it is the only way before us. If you were stranded on an island, a plane or a boat could save you, but if a boat were the only thing coming, you had best get on it.

What makes faith commendable resides in the object of our faith. Faith itself means nothing. Faith in Christ means salvation, glory, and sonship. It is indeed virtuous for man to have faith in Christ, for it is an acknowledgment of God's nature. It is a form of praise and worship. By putting our faith in God we declare that God is a being worthy of our faith. Indeed, to put one's whole faith in anything else is to trust something immeasurably inferior. The praiseworthiness of faith in God is the praiseworthiness *of* God. Through difficult times, turmoil, and life struggles our persistent faith in God is all the more powerful, and all the more commendable because it more greatly reflects the glory and truth of God. That God is greater than all suffering, all sin, all shortcomings, all afflictions, all shame, all hopelessness, all burdens, all pain, all lives, and all worlds. It is a virtue to see past our doubts, to overcome our fears, and to lay aside our anger by trusting in the knowledge of the God that is ever trustworthy and forever faithful.

6

Be Joyful Always: But You Won't Feel Like It

There are moments proselytizing when one feels more like a salesman for Christ, rather than an ambassador. We at times treat the truth like it is a product and Christianity like it is a marketing campaign. We may attend seminars on how to best present our faith, and close the deal. We may speak of salvation in terms of cost-effectiveness, and relationship with God as merely a list of benefits and features of Christian living. Undoubtedly, a key in our selling point is Christian joy. The unrivaled quality of Christian joy is taught loosely and with much vigor. So much so that my wife, having grown up in the church, was quite shocked when first witnessing to nonbelievers to find that they were not all utterly miserable, desperate, or hopeless.

There is of course no biblical principle for suggesting that nonbelievers are devoid of happiness and joy. In fact quite the opposite: sin, the very antithesis of godly living is depicted as pleasurable, though admittedly short-lived. After all, nobody ever engages in sin because they don't like it. The Scriptures clearly indicate that man delights in sin, and in wickedness (Isa 66:3–4). And to have feelings of delight is, by very definition, joy. Therefore, living in open rebellion against God and contrary to his desired will, not only can, but also does in fact elicit the emotion of joy. This is a rather nasty little fact that we may quash with qualifiers. We may say that those who experience joy in that manner are not experiencing *true* joy, that is, the joy experienced in rebellion against God is lesser than the joy that is found in obedience to God. Or we may say that such joy is not *fulfilling* or is ultimately *unsatisfying*. Such stipulations are certainly warranted, but we would do well not to belittle the very real joy man feels in rebellion against God, for to deny man's relish of sin denies the degree of his depravity. Man does not unfailingly continue to sin because he is incompetent. He is not simply a well-meaning fool. The wickedness of man is that he commits sin, certainly, but worse is that he relishes it.

Still, even for the worst of us not all experience of joy is wrapped in sin. The same sorts of things that believers rejoice in, like friends, and family, and fellowship induce much of the nonbeliever's joy. This is a testament to the graciousness of God that rain falls on the righteous as well as the unrighteous (Matt 5:45). Yet for those in a bubble of Christendom, this seemingly self-evident truth is often presented skewed. We speak of joy in Christ as so unrivaled that all other joy appears inauthentic. Although joy is difficult to quantify, I am not of the mind that non-Christian joy is counterfeit, nor emotively lesser. In fact I see no reason why a nonbeliever cannot experience the emotion of joy to the very same degree as Christians, other than the fear that such an admission might expose a weakness in our product. To argue that Christian joy is superior because of its emotive quality is problematic, for there are many things that can bring joy. A woman might find joy in discovering a ring box; an infant might find joy in a rousing game of peek-a-boo. With such a wide range of potential joy suppliers it is quite impossible to demonstrate that Christian joy is the most gratifying or consistent, and so to use Christian joy's emotional gratification as proof of its supremacy is ill founded.

That is not to say that Christian joy is not uniquely exceptional, but that the true superior nature of Christian joy is not in the greatness of the emotion's intensity, but in its source. It is not that Christians *feel* a greater sense of joy, it is that what elicits the joy in us is by nature greater. Let us put it this way; let's suppose that if joy could be measured in units, the joy experienced by the woman contemplating proposal and marriage was found to be equal to the level of joy the child experienced in the game of peek-a-boo. If that were the case, we would still not regard the joy of the woman and the joy of the child as equals even if emotively they were, because emotions aside, the union between a man and woman is by nature greater than a child's game. Though the child's emotions are certainly sincere and deeply felt, they are nevertheless inferior for their source is lesser. In the same way Christian joy is superior, not because it is more authentic, or more frequently or intensely felt, but because the source of Christian joy is Christ, and in comparison to almighty God all other springs of joy are as jejune as peek-a-boo.

The nonbeliever may experience sincere, authentic joy, to the very same emotional level as the believer, but the derivation of their joy is inferior. They are delighting in something that is lesser. Our joy is superior, because it is derived from *the* supreme. I believe we would do better in proselytizing to argue the supremacy of God, rather than the supremacy of our emotions. I do not see how it is persuasive to tell a nonbeliever who claims to be happy that they are *really* or *ultimately* not, particularly when we have no objective means of quantifying such a claim. What is more, I have no intention of cheapening the truth-value of Christianity by rendering it merely an anti-depressant. If the tenets of Christianity invoke nothing but emotions of gloom and melancholy we should nevertheless embrace them fully, for they are true.

Joy is peripheral, not paramount. It is the fruit of a Christian life, not the root of it. Many have faltered by believing that God has called them solely to a life of happiness and have falsely justified every wrong, selfish, and sinful act under a banner of Christian joy. Indeed, the great danger of believing that Christian joy is emotively superlative is that the word of God will be forsaken for the whims of your emotions as the guide for righteous living. One's emotions are not righteous and holy simply because they are powerful, and we are called to holiness not happiness. Though I have no doubt that God wishes you to be happy, he would much prefer you be holy. Now the two are not mutually exclusive. There is joy in righteous living; there is joy in pleasing our Lord. But if your own pleasure is the end goal, there are far easier ways to go about it. After all, one does not become an Olympian and subject oneself to a grueling regiment for the goal of joy, for one can find joy in most anything, but there is only one way to obtain an Olympic medal. It is the prize Olympians seek; the joy is but the consequence of obtaining it. The Christian walk is difficult, and such a hard path is not taken for mere joy, but rather, it is taken so that we may receive the prize: restoration and eternal relationship with God, and joy is only the upshot.

It is a funny thing that those who make the emotion of joy the focus of their life are the most without it. The reason becomes more clear when we begin to define joy. It is such a simplistic word that it is difficult to find truly helpful definitions. We all understand it to be a pleasant or happy emotion, but I think that joy is better understood, not by what it is, but by what causes it. Though there are seemingly endless sources of joy, the trigger is universal: joy is the occurrence when we receive what we passionately desire. Now if a person's primary desire is for joy itself, then they passionately desire to receive something that they passionately desire, which presents a rather glaring problem. If you passionately desire joy more than anything else in existence, then nothing in existence can offer it to you. If you desire joy more than people, then no relationship can satisfy. If you desire joy more than possessions, then no purchase will ever be enough. If you desire joy more than good work, then no vocation will ever truly fulfill. If joy is your goal then everything else becomes bait and if everything else is bait, what is there to ensnare? Those who make joy primary and everything else secondary have less joy because they have devalued all possible suppliers *of* joy. There is simply not much joy in receiving what you do not passionately desire. In this way, those who passionately seek things other than joy, are more likely to have it than those who make joy their prime desire.

Regardless of whether we have much joy or little joy in our lives, we have all experienced the diminishment of joy. Almost immediately upon receiving what we have passionately desired the joy begins to dwindle and fade. It is sometimes astounding how quickly euphoria vanishes, and we are left bewildered as to why it cannot be sustained. The ebbing of joy particularly vexes the Christian, for we tend to attribute the fleetingness of it to the shortcomings of its source. It fits very well into our paradigm that non-Christians are insatiable for they have not turned to the living water. But, what of us? Why is it that we, who have turned to the ultimate source of joy, are still at times unsatisfied?

The good reason, though not the most common, is that the Christian remains, to a certain degree, unsatisfied because he has not yet received what he passionately desires. Though he may take great joy in what he has received, that is, a promise of what is to come and a deposit guaranteeing it, what has been received will not quench. It was never meant to. As C. S. Lewis wrote, "If I find in myself a desire which no experience in this world can satisfy, the most probable explanation is that I was made for another world."[1] If it is the other world that satisfies, you will not have it, until you have at last entered into that other world. So we should not necessarily be discouraged when we at times lack contentment, for the race is not yet won, and the prize not yet garnered, and our true homeland not yet entered. The measure of our joy will not be complete until we receive in full what we arduously desire.

1. Lewis, *Mere Christianity*, 136–37.

If then, a wholly proper response in this life is a certain degree of discontentment, what are we to make of the admonishment to "be joyful always"? (1 Thess 5:16). It is, after all, only natural to feel other emotions in striving for a goal that is so protracted. Our Lord himself seems to express such a sentiment saying, "O unbelieving generation . . . how long shall I stay with you? How long must I put up with you?" (Mark 9:19). Such words do not strike this reader as joyful. In fact there is much in Christ's words and deeds ranging from his biting criticisms, to the temple outburst, to the painful prayer in Gethsemane that do not seem infused with joy. Constantly holy and right though Christ's emotions must be, they are not *prima facie*, at first sight, incessantly joyous.

The reality is emotions are not incessant. They ebb and flow and change, and although we can control them, stunt some and foster others, we do not manufacture them. Our natures respond to stimulus, which produces in us emotion, and it is our conscience and character that tells us which is of the sin nature, and which is of the Spirit, which to spurn, and which to encourage. We may *alter* our feelings by our behavior, but a command not to *feel* x is as impossible to follow as a command to never feel thirsty. Should we then regard the Apostle Paul's words as humanly unattainable as we do Christ's mandate to "be perfect"? (Matt 5:48). Perhaps, but if we do so, we must change our perception of the life of Jesus. For if a mark of perfection is the incessant feeling of joy, Christ, who was perfect, must also have been unceasingly emotionally joyful. Either our perception of Christ's emotional state is not fully accurate or we are misunderstanding what the Apostle Paul means. Or both.

The clearest disclosure of Jesus' emotional state is found on the night of his betrayal. He says, "My soul is overwhelmed with *sorrow* to the point of death" (Matt 26:38, Mark 14:34; emphasis mine). Here, Jesus candidly reveals his current feelings and describes them as sorrowful, not joyful. Very rarely (in fact I am unaware of any study) is the statement of Jesus' emotional condition ever juxtaposed with Paul's charge to be joyful always. Obviously there is an apparent contradiction; if our Lord who is perfect is not always joyful, why must we be?

Curiously, the author of Hebrews provides us another account of Jesus' tremendous ordeal, which states, "Let us fix our eyes on Jesus, the author and perfecter of our faith, who for the *joy* set before him endured the cross, scorning its shame, and sat down at the right hand of the throne of God" (Heb 12:2; emphasis mine). Though this may seem to compound the apparent contradiction, I think it in fact illuminates our quandary. We have been thinking of feelings as singular, as though for any one moment there is only one emotion, and of course this is not so. This is most clearly observed in the relationship between a parent and their child. A parent may feel joy and sadness simultaneously when their child moves out of the house, or gets married, or simply becomes more independent. They rejoice because their child is maturing and becoming an adult, and yet simultaneously they are saddened because their stewardship over the child is ending.

In any single moment there may be a plurality of feelings, and this is not a contradiction. We have said that joy is the occurrence when we receive what we passionately desire and in Gethsemane there are two distinct things that Jesus arduously desires. The first is that Jesus desires not to suffer on the cross, "My Father, if it is possible, may this cup be taken from me," this he does not receive and he is filled with sorrow. The second is that Jesus desires his Father's will, "Yet not as I will, but as you will," this Jesus does receive and he rejoices in it (Matt 26:39). The plurality of emotions, we all experience and can all attest to, harmonizes the apparent contradiction and illuminates how one may have an array of feelings and yet always be joyful.

The Apostle Paul is right to charge that we should always be joyful, for joy should always be a component in the synthesis of our emotion. As Christians we ought to unwaveringly, incessantly, adamantly, and arduously desire the kingdom of God, and God's sovereign will in this world and in our lives. As such, the good Christian never fails to receive his due joy, since his desire cannot be thwarted, for God's Kingdom is constantly furthered, God's sovereignty never shaken, and his will never subverted. As long as Christians desire the things of God, joy will be their constant companion, for the things of God are immutable, everlasting, and freely given.

Jesus, our perfect model, indicates that it is not in itself sin to have differing emotions to joy, and I see no wrong in sadness, anger, or an assortment of feelings, if appropriately applied. Becoming more like Christ does not mean limiting our emotional parameters to one single emotion, for there is not one emotion that is righteous in every context. Rather, as we begin to strip away the old nature and become more like Christ, we will begin to naturally respond with the right emotion for every situation.

Though there is no single emotion or feeling we may call righteous in every context, there is however, one emotion that is wrong for the Christian in any circumstance, and that is despair. It is never righteous for the believer to feel despair, for despair is the complete and utter lack of joy and hope. To have despair in view of almighty God, and the work of Jesus, and the presence of the Spirit is blasphemy. No matter the context, no matter the situation or circumstance, to see the faithfulness of God, to hear of God's promises made to us, and to respond with despair is a sin most egregious. If we were to state the Apostle Paul's words to be joyful always in the negative it would be, "never ever despair."

Now some Christians, rightly recognizing that despair is profanity against the character of God and his divine work, further extrapolate that, in view of salvation and eternity, it is wrong if joy is not the *predominant* emotion for the Christian. They do not deny that you will experience a plurality of emotion; they simply insist that joy must be the main emotion. How can one be, let us say, predominately sad, if we have received the forgiveness of sins and salvation? In light of reconciliation with God everything else is a mere triviality, and so they reason that it is wrong to have a stronger emotional reaction to something else in our lives, for it appears to them to undermine the greatness of the work of God and the joy we have in our redemption.

No good Christian wishes to appear emotionally ungrateful to the sacrifice of Christ. If today we feel more sadness over say, some hurtful words of old so and so, than joy in the work of Jesus, are we being spiritual ingrates? I certainly admit that nothing in this world can compare to the eternal assurance we have in Christ, but I do not think that the interchange of presiding emotions is a recantation of that. In this, I make my appeal in Jesus. In Jesus, the predominant emotion does not always appear to be joy. Just read back over the previous texts we have cited. Does the central feeling shown in Jesus appear to you as joy? If we are to be Christ imitators it seems that to be predominately joyful is not a part of that imitation. Now an argument could be made that the dominance of joy Christians should have is one of the ways in which we differ from Christ. We of course cannot be exactly like our savior, for Jesus is God and we are not, Jesus is perfect and we are not, and perhaps therein lay the reason for emotive divergence. Jesus in his perfection is not a recipient of grace, and so the joy that comes from receiving grace is exclusive to us. Perhaps it is that type of joy that necessitates for us the perpetual dominance of joy in our emotional cocktail.

That is certainly a possibility but I am hesitant to embrace such a view for a couple of reasons. For starters, it is not a common thing to be righteous in diverging from the example of Jesus. If we are to do so we had better have a darn good reason. In this case, the only reason is that we do not wish to diminish the significance of the grace we have received, which is a fine reason, but it must be firmly demonstrated that having dominant emotions other than joy does in fact diminish what we have received. I do not think that it does. If a man received news that his test for a deadly cancer came back negative and while exiting the doctor's office he accidentally fell and broke a bone, would he then pick himself up, dust himself off, and say, "Well I'm off to celebrate now"? Of course not, he would drop everything and focus his thoughts and energy on taking care of his fractured bone. This does not impugn the greatness of being cancer free, nor does it suggest that the man values a single bone more than the whole body. Being cancer free does not make his nerves unreceptive to stimulus, and gaining salvation does not render our feelings unresponsive to other stimulus either. Just because you may occasionally have a stronger emotional response to something more trivial than salvation (and what isn't more trivial?) does not mean you regard salvation as trivial.

Furthermore, if joy must always be predominant then that would mean that a dominant feeling of joy is the right response for any given context, and that seems unreasonable. It is more likely that we should, like Jesus, react differently to different situations. This does not mean we somehow have lost sight of the greatness of salvation or the forgiveness of sins. On the contrary, there are a plethora of emotions that are heightened and encouraged in view of God's mercy and grace, not just joy. A righteous anger, for instance, in the face of sin can be a greatly enhanced emotion in light of the cost of our salvation. I submit that the righteous feeling that should preside is not always joy. If we sin against God, I cannot think that the predominant emotion we should feel is joy. Should it not more rightly be remorse? And from remorse bring us to repentance, and from repentance, joy in forgiveness? Compassion, love, anger, sorrow these are distinct emotions from joy, and though we may have joy in their practice, they are not synonymous with joy, they are their own and they have their own part to play. There is no single proper emotion, dominant or otherwise, there is merely the right emotion for the right situation.

Some may say that arguing for the predominance of joy is not meant to imply that joy should always be the dominant emotion felt, but rather that joy should be the most *consistently* dominant emotion felt. In my view, this is a more reasonable position, as it appears far more compatible with the account of Jesus. But the question becomes, why should one be consistently predominately joyful? If we acknowledge that it is permissible, and more than that, *appropriate* to have different dominant emotions for particular circumstances, then how can we argue for consistency? To say that joy should be the most consistent dominant emotion is to say that your life situations will more consistently warrant joy, and who is to say that? If the righteous and appropriate response to situation x is a dominant emotion different than joy and if you experience more x situations than any other in your life, then it would be *wrong* to be consistently dominantly joyful. If it is in fact *righteous* to respond to certain situations with a dominant emotion other than joy, and you face those situations more consistently than any other situation, you must respond more consistently with a dominant emotion other than joy, for not to do so would be unrighteous.

Now I would say that the reality is it is unlikely that you should have a life that does not warrant predominant joy. And praise be to God for that. I believe that for most Christians the appropriate and righteous response is more often than not joy. I think that is the reality from having an all-powerful God, who loves us and gives us good things. But that is providence, and there is a difference between being joyful in principle and joyful in providence. The principle is not to be predominately joyful, even though that may be the reality; the principle is to respond righteously in your emotions. The reason for this distinction is that if we think that we should be predominantly joyful in principle, we may get the false impression that joy is somehow a more righteous emotion than others. This, in turn, may lead us to believe that other dominant emotions are less holy and therefore have no appropriate expression, which is not true. While living in a fallen world with death, decay, and pain, engulfed by sin and injustice, surrounded by those who hate God and despise his commands, it is wholly appropriate, entirely expected, and right at times to have dominant emotions that are not joy.

In my view the levy to always be predominantly joyful is an unnecessary amendment to the Apostle Paul's words. Joy need not be always dominant, but it must always be. "Rejoice in the Lord always" (Phil 4:4), we are told. Indeed, no matter the circumstance we always have cause to take joy in our Lord, for the righteous response to our relationship with God is joy. The psalmist writes, "You fill me with joy in your presence, with eternal pleasures at your right hand" (Ps 16:11). For those who rightly delight in God their joy shall be everlasting, for God is everlasting. And yet, we will have other emotions, in part because our desire is not yet fully attained, and in part because there are things in this world that should not stimulate joy.

In the picture of the new Heaven and the new Earth we are presented with the fulfillment and completion of joy, where we have at long last achieved our goal and see God face to face in the fullness of his glory. And those things, which rightly hinder our joy, are no more. The Scriptures declare, "There will be no more death or mourning or crying or pain, for the old order of things has passed away" (Rev 21:4). Joy has been perfected, all antagonists are gone, everything that hinders what we passionately desire is stripped away when our natures are fully transformed to desire what is righteous, and what is evil no longer exists to stimulate. The perfected joy of heaven is not a chemical alteration that makes us feel more joyous, as if it were some sort of drug; rather, it is the natural and only possible response to experiencing perfection in reality.

I earlier said that some Christian discontentment in this world is due to the longing for that perfected world, that homeland not yet entered. I believe that is a righteous discontentment, a holy ambition, but it is not, I am afraid, our common discontentment. More often we fail to, as the Apostle Paul put it, "live up to what we have already attained" (Phil 3:16). We are not, at least I am not, joyful when we should be, when the righteous response is joy. The most likely reason you and I do not have joy is that we have ceased passionately desiring the things of God, and have turned to desire the things of the world. The Apostle James skewers the guilty soul saying, "You want something but you don't get it. You kill and covet, but you cannot have what you want. You quarrel and fight. You do not have because you do not ask God. When you ask, you do not receive, because you ask with wrong motives, that you may spend what you get on your pleasures" (Jas 4:2–3). God's sovereign will cannot be thwarted, and so when we desire the things of the world and of our own hearts that are contrary to the things of God, we are destined for disappointment and discontentment. There is not a more miserable creature than the devil.

As we begin to become more like Christ, we will begin to have the desires of Christ, and begin to respond emotionally as Christ would. Until we are made perfect in Christ, we should not expect that every feeling we have will be righteous. Our old nature will continue to pop up, and we must do what we can to swat it back. There is no expectation that you will feel no wrong feelings, for your nature is your nature, and God is in charge of changing that. What we are in charge of is how we react to our emotions, and to our nature. If, when presenting our emotions before God we realize we ought to be joyful and are not, then we should do what joy would do. We may not feel rightly but we must train ourselves to be sons of God by practice. One may be loving without feeling love, one may be compassionate without feeling compassion, one may give without feeling generous, and yes, one may be joyful without feeling joy. We do this by doing what joy impels, just as we do with compassion, grace, and love, even if we don't *feel* like it. What then does joy do? It prompts us to worship, it prompts us to pray thankfully, it helps us to be patient; how quick tempered we are in a foul mood, how gracious we are in joy.

If we are not joyful when we should be, then we must do the things that joy prompts. We must be patient. We must worship God, we must pray and offer thanks to God for that is what joy prompts. You cannot manufacture how you feel but you can determine how you behave. If you wish to feel as Christ feels, you must start by walking in his footsteps. You cannot change what you feel until you change what you are. Act like Christ: practice the things of God and by doing so become more like him in deed, in thought, and in feeling. Then you will be righteous in all ways, and your joy will be made complete.

7

God Provides All Our Needs: But Some Are Homeless And Starving

THE ALL-ENCOMPASSING PROVISION OF God is a Christian percept that when considered from a distance appears so obvious that further inspection seems unwarranted. Of course God supplies all our needs, God supplies our very life and breath, what could be more evident to the believer? But like all subjects, it is less simple the closer you look. It is perfectly true that what makes the light bulb go on, is the light switch, but that is a far cry from the deeper workings for illumination. God's provision is equally plain until we actually pop open the hood and try to explain how it all works.

There is a quote that is often erroneously attributed to Scripture, which claims, "God helps those who help themselves." No doubt this citation is in part mistaken for the word of God simply because it happens to make a declarative statement about God, but also I think in part because there is a ring of truth to it. As much as we Christians may profess that God supplies all our needs, there is no expectation in our minds that if we were to sit and do nothing all day everyday, our bank accounts would somehow be filled. We Christians would expect, just as any secularist would expect, that we would soon find ourselves homeless and hungry. Which means at the very least, we are, at some point, responsible for providing our own needs.

We may say that God is *ultimately* responsible, which really tends to mean that God is *indirectly* responsible. God may not directly supply our bank account with money, but indirectly God supplies us with a job, which in turn supplies us with our monetary needs. But of course this only really pushes back the issue. Would God supply us with a job if we didn't bother to seek one? Ah, but now we may say that God supplies us with the *capacity* to look for a job, which indirectly supplies us with a job, which then supplies us with our monetary needs. You see how easy it is and how far we can push God's provision up the causal ladder? God's provision can be reduced almost to absurdity. Since we are not uncaused entities any causal effect we may have can always be indirectly attributed to God as the first cause. Whatever self-acting steps you may take can in this way be given credit to God, as God is the source of all selves.

But to argue that this is the means in which God provides is troublesome, for if God is responsible and worthy of praise for the indirect consequences of his creative initiative, then isn't God also responsible for, and worthy of derision, for the baleful indirect consequences of said creative initiative? If God is to be given sole credit for providing me with a job because he gave me the capacity to find one, is the onus not also on him when I commit sin, because God gave me the capacity to do so? Why should God get credit for the one and not the other?

Of course I do not think that God is in fact culpable, indirectly or otherwise, for our perpetration of evil simply because God gave us the capacity for it. I believe God's hands are clean in this matter and made all the more so in light of his redemptive plan. But let us be consistent in our thinking. If God is responsible for our provision only indirectly by giving us the ability to act for ourselves, then God is responsible for all actions we may take on our behalf, even the poor ones. In an attempt to augment the supremacy of God, or his generosity by depreciating our own role in our lives we inadvertently minimize our sinful actions, and shift the blame to God. To avoid this, we should look more closely and think more carefully about what it means to say that God provides.

When we say that God provides all our needs it does not mean we are free from all responsibility. Though Jesus taught that our heavenly Father feeds the birds, it does not mean they don't hunt. We are responsible for ourselves. Even for that which we are most helpless, our own salvation, we have duty. Knock. Seek, it says. "Work out your salvation with fear and trembling" (Phil 2:12), and "press on toward the goal" (Phil 3:14). For "from everyone who has been given much, much will be demanded; and from the one who has been entrusted with much, much more will be asked" (Luke 12:48). If then we are accountable for something as monumental as our own salvation, how much more so are we responsible for the piddling affairs of this life?

That is why I believe the small minority of Christians who refuse professional medical treatment in favor of divine healing through prayer and petition are in error. It is not that I think any less of God; it is that I do not think that little of man. From the very beginning God gave man responsibility, because man was created in the image of God, and therefore capable of much. Faith does not mean that we pretend we are less capable than we are, and belittling God's image-bearers does not bolster God. In the presence of God we may bow in adoration, kneel in obedience, or stand tall as sons of glory, but we must not hunch as though fearing that our full measure will rival the supremacy of almighty God. It is absurd to think that man must stoop to God.

It is also remarkably inconsistent that those who never seek a doctor have, for instance, no problem calling a plumber. On what basis can one pick and choose which needs God must provide and which needs man is permitted to meet? It reminds me of the joke regarding the man who was stranded on his roof during a massive flood. A rescue boat comes by and offers him assistance, and the man replies, "No thanks, I have faith in God." Another boat comes by, and another, and finally a helicopter, and still the man refuses their assistance preferring instead to rely on God. At last the man drowns and ascends to Heaven, and as he stands before God he asks God why he didn't save him and God replies, "I sent you four boats and a helicopter."

God created us as remarkably capable creatures. In fact that is the very contrast that Jesus draws between the birds and us when he speaks of God's provision. He says, "Look at the birds of the air; they do not sow or reap or store away in barns, and yet your heavenly Father feeds them" (Matt 6:26). The birds must live day to day on what they can find, but man has knowledge and wisdom and can grow his own food, and save it and store it away. We are unique creations blessed with all kinds of abilities, which makes us uniquely capable to meet our needs.

Now let us not trade one error for another, the fact that we are capable and in part responsible for our own needs does not therefore mean that God is reduced to nothing more than a catalyst for our self-sufficiency. That is a non sequitur. We should avoid both extremes: God's provision does not alleviate us from personal responsibility, and our responsibility does not eliminate God's provision. Rather, God provides and we are responsible. For any given need met, there will most likely be an element of our self-provision and an element of divine provision. Such overlap is not unexpected for we, in general, share the same desire. We desire that our needs are met, and God because he cares for us, desires the same. When I feed my cat, I do so because I desire that she be nourished, and my cat eats the food because she also desires to be nourished. Her self-provision and my provision of her are in that way intertwined. Now, if we were to appropriately answer the question, "Who nourished the cat?" we must take into account both my actions and hers. She would not be nourished had I not bought the food and presented it to her, but that I bought the food and presented it to her does not make her nourished. The cat's actions, though unremarkable in comparison to my own, are nevertheless a part of meeting her needs. It was God who provided the manna, but human hands collected it. Even with *miraculous* provision before them, if the Israelites had not performed their unexceptional task, would they not have surely starved to death?

It is much to our honor that God has charged us with task. How remarkable it is that he who lacks nothing, who holds all power in his hands, and is master of all, should enter into partnership *with* man. It is in humility that the omnipotent God withholds his power so that his own creation may possess power of their own and authority with it. It was God's garden, but he gave it to Adam to tend. It was God's design, but the charge to build the ark was Noah's. It was God's work on the cross, but it is our sacred duty to share the good news. God comes three steps, and let us come the one.

I think we have fairly well established that our needs are met by God's provision, and, though perhaps less remarkable, our self-provision as well. But there is some difficulty in parsing God's provision and our self-provision in our met needs, for it is not always clear-cut. It is at times difficult to ascertain what God's role is in meeting our needs. It is easy to cite the provision of the Israelites or other numerous biblical accounts in demonstrating the role of God, but generally such texts are referring to miracles. Now a miracle bears the unmistakable sign of being the work of God, in fact, that is the primary function of miracle, but it is not what is typically implied when we speak of God's provision. We will deal more with miracles in a subsequent chapter, but for now it is important to understand that mere providence is not miraculous. Though miracle and divine providence are both the workings of God, they are different in function and manifestation. A simple way to grasp the distinction may be to recall our earlier joke. The man drowned waiting for a miracle, but God's provision came in a form that was not miraculous. It was providential, not miraculous, and that is what we will most typically find in our lives. This is important to understand because there are people who deny God's provision if it is not miraculous in nature. That is, if it does not bear the unmistakable sign of being from God.

The cynic, upon seeing the at times convoluted interweaving of God's provision and our self-provision, concludes that since our role in our provision is self-evident and God's role uncertain, we are most likely solely responsible for meeting our needs. Whatever needs are met, or gains acquired, we can always plausibly attribute them to our own actions. And if we have no expectation that God will provide, if we do not take some personal responsibility (work, or look for work), then why give credit to God? Why invoke God at all? If God does not provide unless I act, then perhaps it is only my actions that are really providing.

The problem for the cynic is that with mere providence there is always going to be deniability. But this is for good reason, for what makes a man responsible is his capacity; the greater the capacity, the greater the ability, and the greater the responsibility. Now as long as you are partially responsible it will always be plausible that you are totally responsible, and so, for God to remove all plausible deniability he must take away all of your responsibility by stripping you of your capacity. The only way to effectively eliminate all deniability about God's provision, absent miracle, is to eliminate all potential human influence. The variable must be neutralized.

In essence, for God to prove his provision beyond all conceivable doubt, God must take away our ability to self-act. The irony being, if God were to strip us of all our capacity to meet our needs in order to prove his provision, we would then also not have the capacity to *recognize* that God provided our needs. The act becomes self-defeating. In this way there will always be possible doubt, for a mind capable of doubt is a mind capable of self-acting.

The cynic might have a few more objections. We earlier highlighted miracles as effective at demonstrating God's provision without stripping us of our capacity. A question could then be raised. Why is God's providence so commonly non miraculous, when miracles effectively provide for our needs and also *affirm* God's handiwork? The answer to the question is that if miracles were so commonplace then it would cease to affirm God, and it would in fact defeat the very purpose of miracles. For if miracles were ordinary; they would not be miraculous. If the nature of our reality was such that miraculous acts were common, we would give no more thought to it, nor credit to God, than we did the sunrise this morning.

A second objection to my argument could be launched against its degree. It could be characterized as a straw man since most cynics do not argue for such an extreme burden of proof. For most, there is rarely any demand that God remove all possible deniability regarding God's provision. It would be sufficient to demonstrate providence by removing only *probable* deniability. Though this may seem a fair-minded approach it is easily compromised when those who are less fair-minded take great liberties with what is considered probable. One's philosophical presuppositions have the habit of bending one's analysis of what is probable in one way or another. For instance, if you conclude, *a priori* that supernatuarlism is false then the workings of supernatural forces would strike you as exceedingly improbable. Conversely, if you conclude, *a priori* that supernaturalism is true then the workings of such forces would appear to you as highly probable. In order to accurately gauge the probability of divine providence you must first weigh the probability of the foundational worldview. By my estimation, though this is well beyond the scope of this writing, theism is the most probable worldview and Christianity the most probable of that. Under this worldview, we acknowledge that an omnipotent God exists and that he is a God who cares deeply for us. These two facts make the probability of God's provision highly likely. Therefore, based on the grounding of our worldviews, probability is not a sufficient reason for denying the provision of God.

There are far more troubling things, both for the cynic and the unwavering believer, about God's provision than probability. The problem is, we say that God provides and yet there are plenty of people who, recognizing their own responsibility, actively look for work but cannot find it, or who meticulously care for their bodies but are plagued with health problems, or who do everything that is in their power but still day after day go hungry. There is evidence that there are followers of Jesus who are in want or need and that, at the moment, their needs are not being supplied. When things are no longer in our power and we are at the mercy of God, we may find ourselves strangely in want. This does not bode well for a God that we claim provides.

In response to this uncomfortable notion we may lower the bar as to what constitutes *need*. It could be argued that the only legitimate need is our life and breath, and all else would fall under the class of *desire*. We may desire a roof over our head, or food in our bellies, or a place to sleep, but as long as we are alive we may claim that our need is met. Though possibly homeless, starving, and restless, God may still be accredited as the provider of our needs. And even if we should die from the absence of necessary provision in this life, we may still say that God has provided our needs by the hereafter.

I hope you do not think me a lesser Christian if I find this rather strict definition of *need* as somewhat distasteful. Though it is true that some may error in their liberties of what they classify as need, and it is good for us to be mindful of the distinction between need and desire, such extreme stringency does not accurately reflect the character of God. God does not provide by technicality, our God is a God of generosity, and of overflowing blessing. God does not just give; he gives in abundance. We have long since heard that "the Lord is good to all; he has compassion on all he has made" (Ps 145:9). And that "the eyes of all look to you [God], and you give them their food at the proper time. You open your hand and satisfy the desires of every living creature" (Ps 145:14–16). For, "the Lord longs to be gracious to you; he rises to show you compassion" (Isa 30:18). It does not accurately reflect what we know of God to characterize his provision as the bare minimum. Rather, the God as described in Scripture longs to show compassion and grace upon all his creation and is not content with mere preservation, but with richness and fullness of blessing.

Not only is this a biblical concept, but also it is what corresponds to my personal experience. When I talk about God not meeting the basic needs of his followers I do so as hearsay. I have no personal experience of it, nor do I know anyone personally who has. Far from it. I have food, but not just food, I have an assortment of food to satisfy any craving. I have shelter, but not just shelter, shelter with climate control. I have clothes, but not just clothes, multiple outfits, clothes for any occasion. My needs are not only met, but most of my desires as well. I not only have the essentials, but the entirely frivolous, and not only the frivolous, but also the frivolous in high definition. I am not exceptional in this regard, nor atypical in the slightest, but rather, for my countrymen it is decidedly the norm.

It is important that we present a balanced picture of the provision of God. God richly blesses and provides earthly needs in abundance for many, and perhaps most, of his followers, and also, though I bear no personal witness, I believe it is still true that some followers of Jesus struggle daily and go without basic human necessities. If we are to accurately explain God's provision, these two facts must be accounted for.

The crux of the issue is still how we define *need*. When we think of need as distinct from desire or want, we should realize that need is not a value term, it does not give anything meaning or value. A need is simply a requirement for meeting a certain condition or a particular state of reality. To say that human beings need water to survive is an accurate statement regarding the necessary condition for human survival, but that does not mean that water is meaningful, valuable, or important. The fact that something is necessary does not make it important and what is needed is not necessarily what is important.

When we say that God supplies all my needs, we cannot possibly mean that God supplies all requirements for all conditions that involve me. We do not mean *all* possible needs. If I needed four thousand dollars to fix my car, then four thousand dollars would have to be supplied in order to meet the requirement of this particular condition that involves me. But of course we do not expect that God must or will supply me with the money to meet that requirement. And so, if there are some requirements for certain conditions that involve me that God does not meet, then God does not meet *all* my needs in the very literal sense. Most would respond to this by claming that I don't *really* need a functioning car. Fair enough, but notice that we are no longer speaking of need as simply a requirement for certain conditions or particular states of reality. We are talking about needs as *essentials*.

If we were to rephrase we would say that God supplies all our essentials. So the reason I may not receive four thousand dollars is that having a functioning car is not essential. But this raises the obvious question: Essential for what? Having a functional car is *essential* for having a functional car. Presumably, our needs are that which is essential for life. Have we once again a stringent definition of need? Perhaps, but let's notice something here; when we distinguish between what is essential and what is not essential for life, we are making a judgment, and it could very well be that in our analysis we are mistaken as to what is essential.

Let us then bring our appraisals before God to test if they are true. Are food, and shelter, and clothes essential for life? Our Lord says, "I tell you the truth, unless you eat the flesh of the Son of Man, and drink his blood, you have no life in you" (John 6:53). Christ states, "Do not work for food that spoils, but for food that endures to eternal life, which the Son of Man will give you" (John 6:27). For, "life is more than food, and the body more than clothes" (Luke 12:23), and "a man's life does not consist in the abundance of his possession" (Luke 12:15). Jesus is quite adamant that there is something of such deep importance that it renders all perceived needs moot.

We may live in mansions, and eat our fill, and dress in the highest fashion, but unless we enter into the kingdom of God, unless we eat of the body of Christ and drink his blood, unless we clothe ourselves in grace, we will not have life. To the church of Laodicea the Christ said, "You say 'I am rich; I have acquired wealth and do not need a thing.' But you do not realize that you are wretched, pitiful, poor, blind and naked" (Rev 3:17). There is no earthly provision that is sufficient for life; they all inevitably fail. The only essential for life, the only thing that can meet the requirement for life is our reconciliation with God. It is not food, or shelter, or clothes, for millions have died under their shelters with food aplenty in their cupboards and clothes on their bodies. For life we have but one need, and that is the Son of God. And God, as is his nature, gave in abundance, pouring out his Son so that we may have life, and life to the fullest. "He who did not spare his own Son, but gave him up for us all—how will he not also, along with him, graciously give us all things?" (Rom 8:32). Christ met our need.

To think that God is *going* to meet your need is somewhat backwards, for God has already met your need. The Apostle Peter writes, "His divine power has given us everything we need for life and godliness through our knowledge of him who called us by his own glory and goodness" (2 Pet 1:3). Everything we need for life is met in the surpassing work on the cross.

God has met our essential need, not in part but in whole, not by technicality, nor stringent definitions, but in reality by his abundant and overflowing grace. Yet even still, though our essential need is met, God, being a God who blesses, provides for us the nonessential. It is God's good pleasure to give, and so he does, to even a degree that many of us live lives of incredible comfort, though some of us do not. I do not think we need be bothered by this discrepancy, for we have already said that it does us no good to compare our own suffering to another's, and alternatively, it does us no good to compare our blessings to another's. We are all different, and God has every right to treat us differently according to his good plan for us.

After Jesus had just foreshadowed Peter's eventual suffering and death he replies to Peter's question regarding the fate of John by saying, "If I want him to remain alive until I return, what is that to you? You must follow me" (John 21:22). Indeed, that should be our very response to any variation of God's provision amongst his followers. But I would be cautious to judge who is receiving the better blessing. You are not necessarily better blessed because you have more. Though earthly comfort and luxury is a wonderful thing it is not eternal, and very easily our enemy may lull us asleep in our comforts and rob us of our true rewards.

The duty we all have in being blessed, in whatever manifestation that may take, is to bless others. The Apostle John says, "If anyone has material possessions and sees his brother in need but has not pity on him, how can the love of God be in him?" (1 John 3:17). Of family members in need the Apostle Paul sternly states, "If anyone does not provide for his relatives, and especially for his immediate family, he has denied the faith and is worse than an unbeliever" (1 Tim 5:8). Just as we have responsibility to provide for our needs based on our capability, so to, we have duty to provide for our brothers and sisters in Christ according to our means. "From everyone who has been given much, much will be demanded; and from the one who has been entrusted with much, much more will be asked" (Luke 12:48).

If there are Christians who continue to daily live their lives in desperate want or need, are we who live in plenty not responsible in part for failing to meet their need? If we are to fully address why Christians do not have adequate provision it is in part because we who have, have failed to give. That does not take away from God's responsibility, for God is sovereign and firmly in control so that where we fail, grace abounds. But we are partners in the work of God, much to our honor. Therefore we should make every effort to fulfill every duty before us.

How are we to respond to such a charge? Conviction that leads to repentance is surely of God, but for a topic as this there may be undue guilt. That is, we may feel guilt from simply having what others do not, but what you have is from God, and there is no need for shame or guilt from the blessings of God. Our minds may wander to the rich young man that Jesus commanded to sell all he had and give it to the poor. We may draw from that exchange that unless we too sell all we have and give it to the poor that we are also lovers of money. But that is poor exegesis. Nowhere else in Scripture is such a demand ever made of us.

For the rich young ruler, Jesus was highlighting and pinpointing the sin of his life. For us, the command we find is to give, and give generously. In actuality, we would be in error by selling everything and giving it all away. For by virtue of giving away everything we render ourselves in need and become a burden to our fellow brothers. This, we should not do, but rather, we should follow the example of the Apostle Paul. He writes, "We worked night and day in order not to be a burden to anyone while we preached the gospel of God to you" (1 Thess 2:9). "We were not idle when we were with you, nor did we eat anyone's food without paying for it" (2 Thess 3:78).

The obvious application of a God who provides is that we should never be too timid to be generous. We should never be miserly because of worry. We must work for what we have, share with what we gain, and thank our gracious God who has met our essential need in Christ, so that, as with the Apostle Paul, we may be content "in any and every situation, whether well fed or hungry, whether living in plenty or in want" (Phil 4:12).

8

Miracles Abound: But Have You Ever Seen One?

I AM CONVINCED THAT there is no other word in Christian lexicon that is more commonly used as imprecisely as *miracle*. We invoke it to describe the birth of babies, the presence of good fortune, the sparing from greater tragedies, and for every perceived action of God. The very fact that the word is utilized so commonly as a descriptive for what is recurrent is evidence that it is being misapplied.

In the earlier chapter we made the appropriate distinction between divine providence and miracle. The cause of the frequent use of "miracle" in our lexicon is that we tend to use the latter to describe the former. I have no desire to be a sort of semantics policeman, and I have no qualm with using "miraculous" as a synonym for "amazing," so long as we are saying what we mean, and meaning what we say. Do you really mean that the birth of a baby is a *miracle* or are you using the term loosely? Do you interchange "miraculous" and "amazing" for aesthetic reasons, or because you do not perceive a distinction? Most often we will label providence as miraculous, not because it is an actual miracle, but because we desire to highlight the divine authorship. "Miracle" has an obvious divine connotation, and "amazing" does not. The pyramids of Egypt are certainly amazing, but they are not miraculous, nor are they divine. And so we may opt out of employing "amazing" when describing providence in order to better communicate the divine authorship. This is merely the limitation of language, but it has its dangers.

Choosing the right word is not pivotal for simple linguistic snobbery, the peril of using the wrong word is that it conveys the wrong idea. And wrong ideas about God leads to bad theology, and bad theology to idolatry and disappointment. If we are not clear as to how and why we use the words we use, then we have little chance of escaping distorted conceptions. If that which we call miracle is not truly a miracle, we may wrongly conceive that miracles abound and fall into great discouragement and disillusionment when they don't. Let us not impugn the reality of God by our own poor misconceptions, or reject the biblical God in virtue of wrongheaded extra-biblical thought. A false god is not evidence against the true one.

To avoid dangerous misconceptions we must define miracle carefully. A miracle is not simply any act of God. Christ being fully God was divine in all actions, but surely there is a distinction between Jesus walking to Capernaum and walking on water. The authors of Scripture reserve the label of miracle for only certain actions of God. Though God was at work in all cases, the conquest of nations through Joshua is distinct from the tumbling walls of Jericho. The saving of God's people in Esther is different than the saving of Daniel in the lion's den, and the growing of Jesus in wisdom and stature is different than the virgin birth. The Bible does not label everything that God does as a miracle; the authors reserve the term only for certain actions.

Although a miracle is quite easy to identify, in some respects it is difficult to define. Wayne Grudem's indispensable *Systematic Theology* highlights some of the difficulties in appropriately defining miracle. According to Grudem, the shortcoming of the most commonly proffered definitions is the failure to affirm God's providential workings, and unintentionally assume a deistic worldview.[1] That is, a worldview that regards God as a passive observer who does not intervene in the universe. Regarding one of the more promising definitions Grudem writes, "Another definition of miracle is 'an exception to a natural law' or 'God acting contrary to the laws of nature.' But the phrase 'laws of nature' in popular understanding implies that there are certain qualities inherent in the things that exist, 'laws of nature' that operate independently of God, and that God must intervene or 'break' the laws for a miracle to occur. Once again this definition does not adequately account for the biblical teaching on providence."[2]

Fearful of rendering God as merely a detached observer of his created world, Grudem advances his own definition of miracle but makes a rare blunder. He writes, "We may define miracle as follows: A miracle is a less common kind of God's activity in which he arouses people's awe

---

1. Grudem, *Systematic*, 355–56.
2. Ibid., 356.

and wonder and bears witness to himself."[3] Although I am sympathetic towards Grudem's desire to avoid deistic implications, it is an error to reject a good definition in need of qualification for a bad one that does not *define* anything. Labeling miracle as a "less common kind" of activity of God is so broad as to be practically useless. It is like defining a dodo as a "less common kind of bird."

There are many actions of God that would fit into Grudem's definition of miracle that are clearly not miracles. Take for instance the account of Jesus as a boy in the temple courts. The Scripture says, "After three days they found him in the temple courts, sitting among the teachers, listening to them and asking them questions. Everyone who heard him was amazed at his understanding and his answers. When his parents saw him, they were astonished" (Luke 2:46–48). Unless we are to deny the deity of Jesus, this account is clearly an activity of God. Was it an activity that aroused people's "awe and wonder"? Yes, it stated in the text that everyone was amazed and his parents were astonished. Did it "bear witness" to God? Of course it did. Was it a "less common kind" of activity by God? Certainly, this particular activity of God only happened once in all of human history, and it is exceedingly unlikely to ever happen again. Was it then a miracle? No. The author does not label it as a miracle, nor treat it as such. In fact, all of Jesus' teachings are not described as being miracles, though they bore witness to himself, aroused people's awe and wonder, and were uncommon in relation to the rest of God's workings.

In defense of Grudem's definition, I suppose it could be argued that the simple activity of God teaching us is not uncommon and for that reason is not a miracle. But that is only true if we ignore the *means* by which God carries out his actions, which is absurd. It is the means that defines the miracle. It is certainly not an uncommon activity for God to provide our sustenance, but that does not mean it was not miraculous when Jesus fed the multitudes through limited resources. It was the means by which God provided that was miraculous. In the same way, God teaching us is not an uncommon action of God, but teaching us through the bodily person of Jesus of Nazareth on Earth, through audible sound waves is fully unique, and those who bore witness to it are blessed. But, it is not a miracle.

In properly defining miracle it seems to me essential to acknowledge a natural law. Miracles would in fact be *unrecognizable* were it not for the

3. Ibid., 355.

natural law. Grudem's grievance against invoking the law of nature in defining miracle stems from an outdated perception that a natural law would imply a more deistic interaction of God in relation to his creation in the minds of the general populace. But I would say that with the advancements in the computer age the relation between a being and an established law is, now more than ever, more nuanced in the populace.

There are many good analogues to God's interaction with his creation in our present day, but none stand out as well as the video game. Video game developers create entire fictional worlds; they design and place every bit of vegetation, they create creatures and bestow on them behaviors, they craft a physics system and establish it on their worlds. They are in essence the gods of their created games. Now let us imagine, and it is not difficult to imagine, that a computer programmer designed and created a simulation game about the earth, where the player could manipulate the world through various inputs. The programmer could, through the created and established code, interact with his creation. He could manipulate the clouds, grow vegetation, and command in-game animals to perform certain tasks, like hunt or procreate. Indeed, the programmer could be proactively engaged in his created world through numerous ways.

Now, every game world has rules that are designed, created, and sustained by the developer in the written code of the game. If we are to argue by analogy, it is demonstrable that just because there is an established code does not mean that the designer of that code must be distant, or disengaged, or incapable of directly interacting with the game world. The fact that there is an established natural law in our world does not necessitate that God be deistic.

If we carry the analogy further, we will see that there are two means by which the game developer may manipulate the game world. He could manipulate the game world through the in-game protocol (e.g., grow grass here, move clouds there, and so on). Or, the developer may manipulate the game by out-of-game means; he could, for instance, write new code and input it into the game. This gives us a picture of the distinction between God's providential workings and God's miraculous workings, the in-game action and the out-of-game interaction, as it were.

It is quite interesting that even in the fanciful world of video games, with its outlandish physics and bizarre creature behavior, that the special interaction, the manipulation of the game by non-in-game forces is so easily spotted. We recognize order, even in the, at times, absurd order of the video game world, and thereby recognize the manipulation of the game that originates beyond the established code of the world. Grudem is right to call miracles a less common action of God, but what distinguishes its uncommonness is its relation to the natural law. It is unwise to dispense with the natural law in defining miracles because the natural law is how we *identify* miracles.

One more bit of clarification. How we distinguish between what we call the "natural" and the "supernatural" is that the natural is everything that is within the system; in our analogy, it would be the in-game world. The supernatural is everything that is outside of the system; in our analogy, it would be the out-of-game world. Now, it could be misinterpreted that the natural law is the observation of only naturalistic forces, that is, forces caused only by things or beings within the system, or in-game. It could be thought that if it is a part of the natural law, then its cause is necessarily natural rather than supernatural. But the natural law is merely the observed order of our universe, and supernatural forces could, in fact, cause the order. It may be perfectly *natural* or common for our world to be influenced by supernatural forces in certain ways. Again, a miracle is not defined by its cause but by its means. The computer programmer could, through the in-game protocols, click a button and cause rain in the game world. The cause then, of the rain, is a supernatural being, a being that stands outside of the system, but the means of generating the rain is natural, because the rain is produced from within the system. So we may see that just because we call something "natural" does not mean there is no supernatural hand involved. It merely means that what we classify as "natural" was brought about within the system, the in-game protocols.

Having qualified our position, we may now define miracle. A miracle is an intervention of the observed and established laws of nature by a supernatural force in order to manifest or affirm God's presence, power, authority, or proclamation. It is sometimes thought of as a *suspension* of the law of nature, or a *violation* of it, or worse an outright *breaking* of the natural law. But a miracle no more breaks the natural law than added computer code breaks the game. "Suspension," or "violation" of the natural law is also not quite right.

Suppose there was an object that was rolling off a table. We could predict with great accuracy that according to the laws of nature, of inertia and gravity, that the object will roll off the table and fall immediately to the ground. Yet let us say, that as the object was rolling off the table, you reached out and grabbed it. Our prediction based on the natural order was wrong, but at no point was the law of nature ever suspended or violated. Rather, the laws responded in the exact way that they would operate in relation to the added variable.

It is the same with miracles. The natural law responds to intervention by naturalistic forces in the same way that it would respond to intervention by supernatural forces. If the object rolling off the table was suddenly halted in midair, by an invisible supernatural force, it would be a miracle, but it would no more be a breaking, or violation, or suspension of the natural law, than if you or I stopped the object from falling.

There is also some confusion between miracle and revelation. To be sure there are at many times overlap between the two, but the one does not necessitate the other. I have heard many people refer to God's speaking to them as "miraculous," but whether or not it constitutes a miracle depends on *how* God spoke. Did God intervene upon the natural law in order to reveal himself? If the answer is yes, then I see no reason not to label it as a miracle, but if the answer is no, then it seems best to label it as merely revelation. God speaking through a fire engulfed bush that was not being consumed, would certainly be a miracle, but God revealing himself through a dream, as he did with the Apostle John, is amazing and wonderful but not an intervention upon the laws of nature and therefore not necessarily a miracle.

I am afraid that there are some who may feel that I am throwing cold water on all of the perceived miracles that they have had. Who am I, after all, to say that it wasn't a miracle when it feels so darn *miraculous*? It is understandable. A miracle is a special thing, and we all want to be a part of, and bear witness to, something special. But that is not for us to decide; we cannot arbitrarily define what miracle is in order to soothe our egos and prop ourselves up as uniquely blessed by God. We do not get to choose the manner in which God intervenes in our lives. Jesus said, "For I tell you the truth, many prophets and righteous men longed to see what you see but did not see it, and to hear what you hear but did not hear it" (Matt 13:17). We may long to see the power of God displayed through miracle, as the righteous men of old longed to see the coming Messiah, but it is God that chooses how he reveals himself and how he blesses. "If I want him to remain alive until I return, what is that to you? You must follow me" (John 21:22).

A question may arise in our minds. Why is it that miracles appear so prevalent in Scripture and yet so absent in our modern day lives? The compilation of the Bible may at times cause us to lose sight of the actual history. We may forget the hundreds and perhaps thousands of years where no miracle occurs, or at the very least, is not recorded. The Bible is in some ways a highlight reel, and what may have ended up on the cutting room floor are the generations and generations of God-fearing people who never experienced God's miraculous workings.

We do, however, see particular moments in history where miracles abound, where there is a sudden flurry of supernatural activity. The reason for this is that God's use of miracles is intentional and purposeful. The upsurge in miracles is most often connected by a disruption in the status quo. That is, whenever God establishes a new order, or a new law, or a new society, or a new covenant, or a new dynamic in his relationship with creation that departs from the status quo, it is authenticated as being from God, by the presence of miracles. When God established his covenant with Abraham, it was attested by the birth of Isaac born from a woman well beyond her birthing years. When God set apart the Israelites and established with them his covenant, it was authenticated by the presence of miracles when God brought them out of Egypt. When Jesus established the new covenant, it was confirmed by his miracles.

Nicodemus said of Jesus, "We know that you are a teacher come from God; for no one can do these signs that you do, unless God is with him" (John 3:2). In Acts it says of Jesus that he was "a man attested to you by God with mighty works and wonders and signs which God did through him in your midst" (Acts 2:22). The apostles as well were distinguished as being of God by their performance of signs and wonders (2 Cor 12:12). The same may be said of the leaders and prophets of the Old Testament, such as Moses, and Elijah. What you find in Scripture is a consistent pattern that when God moves to alter the status quo, he authenticates it by the manifestation of miracle.

It is helpful to always think of miracles within their historical background and context. Let us think of Jesus; Jesus of Nazareth was such a disruption to the status quo that absent the presence of miracles it would have been difficult, if not impossible, for any God-fearing, first-century Jew to believe in him. Jesus said, "Believe me when I say that I am in the

Father and the Father is in me; or at least believe on the evidence of the miracles themselves" (John 14:11). The miracles authenticated that Jesus was God, and that the new covenant in his blood was from God.

At certain times in human history where there is a dramatic increase in miraculous workings, we will tend to find that God is altering the status quo. The reason we may lack the same degree of miraculous workings in our modern times is that God is not disrupting the status quo. God is not establishing a new covenant, or a new order, or a new society, or changing the way God relates to his followers. That does not mean that miracles are now completely absent, but nor are they haphazard. They are intentional and purposeful, and used with good reason, which means that we should not expect that this age will, or must, experience the same level of miraculous workings as previous ages. Rather, we should acknowledge that there are certain distinct times in human history where it is sensible for certain actions or revelations of God to be authenticated by miracles.

Some may object to my characterization that miracles are less present in this modern age, and they very well may be right. It is difficult to quantify the amount of miraculous events at any given time, but the rampancy of *concocted* miracles is evidence that true miracles are not rife. After all, authentic miracles make for better stories.

We all want to see miracles. We all know that at some point in our lives to get what we want will require a miracle; nothing less will do. There are some prognoses too grave, some circumstances too dire, to be overcome by mere providence, to be solved by the tools of the natural order. We all want to see miracles because the natural law contains things that we would rather do without. The natural order has heartache, and suffering, and goodbyes that come too soon.

This, we should then remember, that the natural order will pass away. We need not look for tangential miracles when we have the knowledge of the miracle of miracles. Lazarus rose from the dead, but only to die again. Manna came down from Heaven, and the multitudes were fed, but only to be hungry again. Such miracles as only *interventions* of the natural law do not eliminate the corruption, and wickedness, and evil that exists within the natural order. Each time miracles came and went but the natural order remained intrinsically unaltered, until the breaking of one dawn, where there was found an empty tomb and a raised living body, and the world has never been the same since.

We need no other miracle than the miracle of Jesus Christ's resurrection, for through this one grand miracle God broke the back of the corrupt natural order. By the miraculous workings of God through the bodily resurrection of Christ we are kept for eternity and spared from the coming destruction. We are saved because God intervened. Where there was death, now there is life, where there was despair, now there is hope. The death and resurrection of Jesus is the ultimate supernatural intervention of the natural law, and we need not look to any other.

9

Prayer Is Effective: But When You Keep Praying Does Anything Happen?

THERE HAVE BEEN SEVERAL scientific studies conducted that have tried to ascertain the effectiveness of prayer. The results have been mixed. In one case a double blind study on 393 patients in the San Francisco General Hospital's Coronary Care Unit concluded that those who received prayer performed better than those who had not. Those who had received prayer required fewer antibiotics, and were more likely to avoid pulmonary edema and death.[1]

Another study, according to the Associated Press, examined 1,800 patients undergoing heart bypass surgery. The patients were divided into three groups. The first group was told that they were being prayed for and were prayed for, another group was told that it was possible that they were being prayed for and were also prayed for, and the final group was told that it was possible that they were being prayed for but were not prayed for. The result was that those patients who were aware that they were being prayed for developed more complications after surgery than those who did not know that they were being prayed for.[2]

These kinds of studies are appealing to the nonbeliever as well as the believer and one side or the other often touts the results of such tests to support their own philosophical prejudices. But I see no real use for these tests because, in addition to their questionable methodologies, such studies fundamentally misunderstand the nature of prayer. They mischaracterize the function of prayer, and it is impossible to demonstrate the effectiveness of anything if you do not know what its function is. You cannot say that something does not work unless you know what its function is.

1. Williams, "Can the Power of Prayer be Proven?" lines 3–9.
2. Associated Press, "Power of Prayer Flunks An Unusual Test," lines 40–45.

When Christians claim that prayer is effective, we mean that it is effective within the context of its function. If we are to accurately judge the effectiveness of prayer, we must be certain that we understand prayer's function. Otherwise, it is like saying that my computer is ineffective, because it does not make toast. But making toast is not the function of the computer.

In scientific studies, often prayer is treated as though it is a magical wish and God a genie. As though a few mumbling of words somehow compels, indeed forces, God's compliance and subjects him to our will. The function of prayer through this understanding is that prayer is a means to coerce God into getting what we want. But of course, through Scripture, we have ample evidence that this is not the function of prayer. David fasted and prayed that God would spare his son, but God did not. Moses prayed that God would allow him to enter into the Promised Land, but he did not. Paul prayed three times that God would remove the thorn from his flesh, but he did not. And most famous of all, Jesus prayed that the cup might pass from him, but it did not.

Still, the idea of the effectiveness of petitionary prayer is not without grounding, albeit with qualification. Jesus flatly said, "If you believe, you will receive whatever you ask for in prayer" (Matt 21:22). Undoubtedly this verse has led to much disappointment, particularly, if it is coupled with the words of the Apostle James who states that "the prayer offered in faith will make the sick well" (Jas 5:15). How often have Christians prayed sincerely believing through faith for healing and yet did not receive? The fine print of prayer is that righteous men have prayed, have begged, have cried out to God, have pleaded, and still have not received. That is the reality.

What then, are we to make of it? We have been told, "the prayer of a righteous man is powerful and effective" (Jas 5:16). We have heard that if we remain in Christ, and his words remain in us, "ask whatever [we] wish and it will be given [to us]" (John 15:17). We might conclude then, that the reason prayer, at times, produces poor results is due to our personal failure. We do not receive because we are not truly righteous, or we are not truly remaining in Christ, or we are not truly believing in God. There is evidence, after all, that the power of prayer is diminished by our shortcomings. The Apostle James says, "When you ask, you do not receive because you ask with wrong motives, that you may spend what you get on your pleasures" (Jas 4:3). He further states, "He who doubts is like a wave of the sea, blown and tossed by the wind. That man should not think he will receive anything from the Lord; he is a double-minded man, unstable in all he does" (Jas 1:6-8). We may recall also that the reason David's prayer did not save his son was a consequence of his sin (2 Sam 12:13-15). And the reason Moses did not receive what he asked from God was a consequence of his disobedience to God (Deut 3:23-25; 32:50-52).

Is the blame for prayer's apparent ineffectiveness to be laid entirely upon our shoulders? Do we not receive what we ask because we are unrighteous, or doubting, or we ask with wrong motives? If that is the sum of it, then petitionary prayer seems rather hopeless. If the problem is the deficiency of our righteousness, we are sunk, for there is "no one righteous, not even one" (Rom 3:10). We all continue to sin, and if that sin prohibits us from receiving what we ask, it seems only natural to grow more doubtful as to the power of prayer, not less. How horrid a thought it is that those who fervently prayed and yet have lost a loved one may now be contemplating that things might have been different if only they were more righteous, or less doubtful. There is a point to be made about our personal deficiencies and the problems of prayer, but praise be to God that, that is not the sum of it.

We have other examples of petitions that were not granted. The thorn in the Apostle Paul's flesh was not removed because Paul was behaving in a way that was unrighteous, or because he was asking with wrong motives, or because he did not have enough faith. Paul's request was simply not in God's will (2 Cor 12:7-10). Even better, we have Jesus praying and not receiving. No one can say that Jesus was unrighteous. No one can say that Jesus doubted too much. No one can say that Jesus asked with wrong motives. Yet when Jesus prayed in Gethsemane that the cup should pass, he did not receive. We may then conclude that our petitionary prayers must be in alignment with God's will in order for our prayers to be granted. The Apostle John indicates this by saying, "This is the confidence we have in approaching God: that if we ask anything *according to his will*, he hears us. And if we know that he hears us—whatever we ask—we know that we have what we asked of him" (1 John 5:14-15; emphasis mine).

So far we have seen that the function of prayer is not mere wish fulfillment, and yet, petitions *are* granted through prayer with certain criteria. Our prayers must be in accordance with God's will, we must be righteous in our prayers, pray without improper motives, and we must believe in faith that God will hear and answer our prayers. Now we should not think that our personal deficiencies in prayer can subvert God's sovereign will. That is, what God has preordained to do will be done regardless of our shortcomings. For how can God's supreme will be subverted? God may still do what the hypocrite babbling in the street corner, praying through false motives asks him to do, if it is in accordance with God's supreme will. The Apostle Paul said, "It is true that some preach Christ out of envy and rivalry, but others out of good will. The latter do so in love, knowing that I am put here for the defense of the gospel. The former preach Christ out of selfish ambition, not sincerely, supposing that they can stir up trouble for me while I am in chains. But what does it matter? The important thing is that in every way, whether from false motives or true, Christ is preached" (Phil 1:15–18). If then, God can bring people to himself through the preaching of the gospel by false motives, then God can certainly answer the prayer offered through false motives, in accordance with his will.

This brings us to one of the most mystifying elements of prayer. I think it is sensible to say that our deficiencies cannot foil God's will. But can our righteous prayers alter it? One of the most curious prayers depicted in the Bible is found in the book of Exodus. The Lord has seen the sin of the Israelites in forming the golden calf and God declares, "'I have seen these people,' the LORD said to Moses, 'and they are a stiff-necked people. Now leave me alone so that my anger may burn against them and that I may destroy them. Then I will make you into a great nation'" (Exod 32:9–11). Moses, we are told, pleads before God, seeking God's favor, and asking that God would turn from his fierce anger and remember his promises to Abraham, Isaac, and Jacob. The Bible then says, "Then the LORD relented and did not bring on his people the disaster he had threatened" (Exod 32:14).

A *prima facie* interpretation of this text would indicate that the prayer of Moses affected God's actions. But does that then mean the *cause* of God's actions was Moses' prayer? Should we then think that if Moses had not uttered those words in prayer, God would have destroyed the Israelites and fulfilled his promise through Moses? The most troublesome quality about this passage is that God is not simply relaying God's emotions, as he did when he grieved over his creation before the flood, but that God is communicating his *intentions*. If it were only God's emotions, we could easily resolve this account by saying that God at this point emotionally desired to destroy the Israelites but willed that they be spared. Alas, the resolution of this account is not that easy.

The fact that God in this account expresses his intentions and then subsequently deviates from those expressed intentions has led some to believe that God can change his mind. That through prayer Moses altered the plan of God, and that we, through prayer can affect God in the same way. Such a notion becomes immediately problematic when we recall declarative statements, as is found in Numbers: "God is not a man, that he should lie, nor a son of man, that he should change his mind" (Num 23:19). And yet there are other passages in Scripture, like the account of Moses or the story of King Hezekiah, in which, at the very least, it strongly appears that God changed his mind, or altered course (2 Kgs 20:1–7). Any simple reading of these accounts presents us with conflicting ideas, though they may not necessarily be irreconcilable.

This is important in answering our question of what the function of prayer is, for the function of petitionary prayer would be greatly altered whether God's mind can be changed, or influenced, or not. If we are to properly determine the effectiveness of prayer, we must correctly identify its function, which means addressing whether or not God can change his mind. We should ask ourselves: What changes a person's mind? There are two primary causes for changing minds; the first is the acquirement of new facts, and the second is the personal, emotional experience of the facts.

A man may decide that today is perfect weather for a day at the beach, but then after hearing from the weatherman that rain is eminent, change his mind. This would be an example of a mind changing by the acquirement of new facts. The man intended to go to the beach, but the acquirement of new evidence, caused him to change his mind. Now let us suppose that a man intended to go to the beach tomorrow morning, and knew all the facts surrounding the excursion. He knew what the weather would be like for the day, he knew what the condition of the beach would be like, and he knew what the traffic would be like in getting there. Having all the facts regarding the excursion the man plans to go to the beach tomorrow, but then in the morning the man wakes up and is suddenly no longer in the mood to go to the beach, and so decides against it. In this case, the man has changed his mind, but not because he has acquired some new facts, but because his emotions have changed regarding the facts.

In the case of an omniscient being, it is clearly impossible for an omniscient mind to be changed based on the acquirement of new facts.

An omniscient mind knows all facts and so cannot be persuaded by any new facts. But can the omniscient mind be changed by the second means, not by information but by emotion? If we were to ascribe true omniscience to the man in our example would he behave in the same manner? If he had all knowledge regarding the excursion to the beach as well as all knowledge regarding his emotional state the following morning, would he still make preparations for going to the beach? That seems unlikely, but not impossible. It would be a futile and silly action, but not a logically impossible one.

Although it may be unlikely for the omniscient man to take active steps in preparing for something he knows he will not do, it is not so unlikely for him to merely express his intentions. There is nothing impossible or necessarily unlikely for the omniscient man to say, "I intend to go to the beach tomorrow, but I will not." His intention in this case is merely reflective of his present desire. It is permissible for an omniscient mind to say today, "I want to go to the beach tomorrow," and yet tomorrow to say, "I do not want to go to the beach." That could easily be labeled as a change of mind, although perhaps more accurately it is a change of heart. Regardless of how we label it, it is still a change and one that has occurred not as a result of a lack of knowledge. For a man with full knowledge can still say, "I want to go to the beach tomorrow, and yet, tomorrow I will not want to go to the beach."

Could it be the same for God? Can the mind of God be changed, not by acquiring new facts, which would be contrary to God's omniscience, but by the changing of his emotions in relation to the facts? This is perhaps the best explanation as to how our prayers can affect an omniscient God, but it faces many objections.

The first objection pertains to how exactly one's emotions can be affected if one has full knowledge. It could be argued that changes in emotions can only really occur through the receiving of new data as emotional stimuli. That is, through our faculties and senses we are constantly taking in new data, and the processing of that data results in our emotional states. Our emotions change based on the processing of changing stimuli. So we may change from happy to sad, if we hear some sad news, or we may change from at peace to angry, if something occurs that angers us. Our emotional state is then tied to an external variable, but if the variable is already known, does it still have an affect? If we are happy, and the external variable, such as "sad news" causes us to be sad, then an omniscient mind that already knows the "sad news" would *already* be sad and would not shift in emotions. The omniscient mind, it is then argued, already possesses awareness of all possible variables and so cannot shift in reaction to them. The omniscient person could not then shift from happy to sad, because there is no saddening cause, or event, or moment that the omniscient mind is not already aware of.

In response to this objection it should be noted that the argument reduces the emotional changes of God recorded in the Bible to mere anthropomorphisms. If there can be no shifting in emotion for the omniscient mind, then God must be in one emotional state for eternity. In my mind that characterizes God as something rather lifeless, but there are other problems with this argument. It makes the mistake of thinking that knowledge, even perfect knowledge, is as potent a stimulus as experienced reality. This is just not the case, and we have good evidence that that is not the case. For instance, a movie that we have seen a hundred times, that we can quote by heart, that we can hum the musical score to, that we can replay scenes from perfectly in our minds, may upon viewing, still bring us to tears. Despite the vastness of our knowledge, the actual experience still has an impact.

We see this in Scripture as well. Jesus had full knowledge of the death of Lazarus, for Christ revealed that fact to his disciples from afar, and yet when Jesus came to the tomb and saw the people he was "deeply moved in spirit and troubled," and wept (John 11:33). Since the very creation of the world, Jesus knew that he was to suffer and die, Jesus after all, predicted it many times, and yet on the night of his betrayal he was filled with sorrow. It is a curious thing, but it seems true that emotions are not fully invoked by the mere knowledge of facts, but by the experience of them. Happy moments are still happy, and sad moments are still sad, whether or not we have full knowledge of every happy or sad moment. There is nothing prohibiting, even an omniscient mind, from appreciating the distinction between what is merely known, and what is actualized. Indeed, if that distinction were not recognized, such a mind would not be omniscient, and therein lays the possibility for emotional divergence. The omniscient mind is free to respond differently to foreknowledge, and the actualization of that knowledge, precisely because there *is* a difference.

In this way, it is possible that our petitionary prayers may affect God's emotions by the actualization of the prayer. Certainly God already

Prayer Is Effective: But When You Keep Praying Does Anything Happen?

knows what he is going to do, and he already knows what you are going to say, but the reality of saying it still has an impact. The Apostle James says, "You do not have because you do not ask God" (Jas 4:2). The implication seems clear, if we do not get because we do not ask, then our asking must in some way influence God's actions. It cannot be that our prayers influence God by informing him, for God knows all things, as Jesus said, "your Father knows what you need before you ask him" (Matt 6:8). Therefore, if God is to be influenced at all, it must be that the actualization of our prayers influences his emotions.

I think that the argument we have outlined has successfully thwarted our first objection, but in the minds of many it is no closer to being accepted. For many the idea that God may be influenced or swayed by emotions is a distasteful notion. It conjures in the mind visions of God as a basket case who can be emotionally manipulated by simply pushing the right buttons. As if the right sob story, or the right turn of emotional appeal may trick God into giving you what you want. This is not so much a formal objection to the argument as it is a visceral rejection of it, and in that way, it is perhaps more potent.

We must be quick to remember that God's emotions are always perfectly holy, perfectly righteous, and perfectly appropriate in every situation. It is not as if God's sovereign will could be thwarted by any amount of sobbing or pitiable displays. God cannot be manipulated, for any attempt to manipulate is easily spotted by the omniscient mind. Hence, the Apostle James makes the statement about asking with wrong motives. God's emotions flow from his character and his character is immutable. God's immutable character is particularly important because it prevents us from suggesting that God's shifting emotions are arbitrary.[3] That is, we have no reason to think that God would feel x about one situation, and then given time, would feel z about the very same situation. There is no danger that God would, let us say, feel anger towards sin, but at another point feel happy regarding sin. Rather, God's emotions shift

---

3. Curiously, in the same area of Scripture in which we hear that God's mind does not change like man's, we are presented with a bizarre encounter with Balaam and his donkey. Balak summons Balaam, and God tells Balaam to go to Balak. The next morning when Balaam sets out, God is described in Numbers 22:22 as being very angry, and an invisible angel of the LORD is prepared to strike Balaam dead. There seems to be a rather radical shift in God's emotional stance that is unaccounted for. However, that does not mean we should consider it as arbitrary; there is a righteous reason, but the reason is simply not known.

when the circumstances shift. Our prayers may affect God, because the actualization of the prayers changes the situation. God is free to feel differently about different situations, precisely because they are different, but God cannot feel differently about the exact same situation.

The final objection to the argument thus far has perhaps been ruminating in the back of your mind for some time now. In discussing the affect that prayers have on God it is impossible to talk about it free from invoking time language. Cause and effect are fundamentally tied to sequence, which is the very essence of time, and shifting emotions would connote a "before" and "after," which only makes sense in a temporal world. But there is a strong tradition that God is timeless, that God stands outside of time. It is certainly a Christian shibboleth that God is timeless, but the biblical input is inconclusive. As Dr. William Lane Craig argues in his book, *Time and Eternity*, "A literal reading of the biblical texts gives the overriding impression that God is eternal in the sense of existing at all times, not in the sense of being timeless."[4]

Without a concrete biblical pronouncement of the exact nature of divine eternity, we are free to hypothesize God's relation to time. In his book Craig makes a rather compelling argument that God was perhaps timeless before creation and at creation is temporal. As Craig put it, "Given the reality of tense and temporal becoming, the most plausible construal of divine eternity is that God is timeless without creation and temporal since creation."[5]

Craig's conclusion is perhaps most appealing because it provides a framework for understanding how God relates to his creation, as God is accredited as doing. It seems to me, that the greatest problem of thinking that God is timeless, is that timelessness implies, as far as I reason, a sort of stasis. It seems impossible for change to occur in a timeless realm, for any variation would indicate a *time before* the variation and *after* the variation. Any kind of change, big or small, can only find expression in temporality, for any kind of change conveys a *before* (the change) and an *after* (the change).

Any sort of understandable expression of timelessness must be free from transitions, or changes, or alterations. Yet, Christian doctrine expresses a fundamental change that occurred through the incarnation of the Son. God became man. But the very act of *becoming* indicates that

4. Craig, *Time And Eternity*, 239.
5. Ibid., 241.

the Son was not always fully man as he is fully God. A straightforward reading of Scripture would in no way convey that the Son was, before creation, fully man. Rather, the Bible says, "Being in very nature God, did not consider equality with God something to be grasped, but *made himself nothing, taking the very nature of a servant, being made in human likeness*" (Phil 2:6–7; emphasis mine). If God took on the nature of man, as the Bible suggests, then a change occurred within the Godhead. We can chronicle *before* the incarnation and *after* the incarnation, which implies that God is within time.

Some may protest this and appeal to God's mystifying nature. Although we cannot understand how change can occur in timelessness, this does not mean that God is not timeless. The true understanding of timelessness may be simply beyond all our comprehension. Indeed, I certainly appreciate the fact that God's greatness and vastness is beyond our full comprehension, and that there are many things we do not understand about God's nature. But why should we cling to God being timeless with creation, which is a view we do not understand and that has no special claim to scriptural support, when we have an explanation that *is* understandable, coherent, and fully compatible with Scripture? God being more unintelligible for the sake of being unintelligible does not make him greater.

We have come a long way, and are closer to understanding an aspect of prayer. We have seen how it is possible that our prayers may affect God. The actualization of our prayers changes the situation, and God responds differently, and appropriately, to different situations. Though not technically a change of mind, and what God has resolved to do he will do, nevertheless, our prayers can still influence God's actions.

We have been looking at petitionary prayer, because it is an important element of prayer, and because it is the most difficult aspect of prayer. But it is certainly not the only aspect of prayer, and if we are going to understand the function of prayer we have to take into account other aspects of prayer. There are other prayers, there are prayers of thanksgiving, and there are prayers of repentance. It is funny how no one seems to question the effectiveness of a prayer of thanksgiving. The other aspects of prayer really highlight the fallacy of our thinking about prayer. We think of it as a cause, and prayer is not a cause, it is a means. It is the means for us to petition God, it is the means for us to influence God's actions, it is the means for us to praise God and thank him, it is the means for us to ask for forgiveness, it is a means for us to grow more like God, it is a means for us to communicate with God.

The purpose and function of prayer is to serve as a means for us to communicate with almighty God. And through Jesus' name, our mediator, it is always effective. It always works. Let us not gloss over the reality of what prayer really is: it is the way we can communicate to *God*. We, lowly we, have the ear of the creator and sustainer of all things. It has been said that if we *really* knew the effectiveness of prayer we would pray more. I submit that if we *really* knew who God was, we would pray more.

Now the fact that we can communicate with God certainly has implications; we can petition and those petitions can be granted, we can ask for forgiveness and be pardoned, but to say that prayer is strictly the cause of those results is like saying my phone causes a cab to arrive at my doorstep, and from that extrapolate that the function of a phone is to get cabs. Through prayer many things can be achieved, just as many things can be done through a phone, but those results are not strictly the function of either.

What we can say is that prayer is communication with God, and that by Jesus it is always effective. Because prayer works, we have the ear of God and we can ask things of him. Sometimes God will grant us what we ask and sometimes he won't. At times what we ask is contrary to God's supreme will, and other times we ask from improper motives and evil desires. There is no guarantee that God will always do what we ask, but there is assurance that God will always listen.

We should always continue to pray, if for no other reason than because of the exceeding greatness of he whose ear we have. One of the greatest results of prayer is that by communicating with God we become more like him. When we petition God, and wait patiently for God's answer, we grow spiritually. When we thank God and praise him, we become more aware of the character of God and align ourselves more in his will. When we pray for others, and for our enemies, we learn how to love as God loves. We become more and more like God, more and more righteous, more and more in tune with his will, and then we may ask what we want and it will be given, for it is what he wants.

10

In Everything Glorify God: But Life Seems Indifferent To Glory

It is quite universally acknowledged by Christians that the purpose of our lives is to glorify God. We rightly recognize that the glory of God should be our highest aspiration. And yet much of our days, and perhaps most of our days, are spent in activities that we would most likely describe as being indifferent to glory. It is not as if we would characterize our time and actions as being inglorious to God, but neither would we say that they are particularly glorifying of God.

The charge that whatever we do should be done "for the glory of God," as is often cited from 1 Corinthians 10:31, can be a very discouraging thing. We eat, we sleep, we watch television, we read books, we play sports, we play games, we surf the web, we clean our house, we clean our cars, we shower, we shave, we put on make-up, we do our chores, we work our jobs, we shop, we do a seemingly endless amount of tiny little things that seem spiritually vapid.

Even if we were to argue that many of our mundane actions really do glorify God, it still seems self-evident to us that there are things we could be doing that would bring *more* glory to God. Instead of watching television, couldn't we be reading the Bible? Instead of spending time on our hobbies, couldn't we start a ministry? Instead of seeing what's happening on Facebook, couldn't we meditate on God? Well the answer to these questions is yes, because the answer is always yes. There is always more that can be done, and better ways to use our time. If we take thirty-minute showers we could cut them to twenty and give ten more minutes to reading God's word. Or if they must be thirty minutes at least we could be praying the whole time. We may enjoy eight hours of sleep, but we could get by on five, and wouldn't that extra time be better spent in mediating on God?

Taken to the extreme it becomes very clear that even the most zealous for God's glory must draw a line somewhere. The full application of the principle that certain actions bring God *more* glory than others leads to absurdities. If we really believe that praying is more glorifying to God than sleeping, then those of us who truly desire to glorify God should dedicate ourselves to fewer and fewer hours of sleep. I imagine that the added hours of prayer gained from such behavior would be spent petitioning that the good Lord would keep us awake.

Now some may take this to mean that in our frail form it is impossible for us to glorify God as we should. Although we may not be able to glorify God fully at present, a time is coming when we will shed all our frailties, and need neither drink, nor food, nor sleep, and then at last, we will be able to glorify God in all ways to the full measure. There is a good deal of sense in thinking that our glorifying of God will be perfected at the resurrection, but it is our depravity that must be reconciled to perfection, not our humanity.

Human beings need food and need sleep, and none of those actions are inglorious to the one who created them. We know this to be so, for Christ, who perfectly glorified the Father, slept and ate, and practiced carpentry. I suppose it could be hypothesized that Jesus through those "less glorifying" actions was praying or meditating the whole time. Perhaps even in sleep, the God nature of Jesus was fully engaged in other more fitting spiritual endeavors. But that is such a radical and contentious construal of Scripture that even hypothesizing it is embarrassing.

However, if all these banal activities we are engaged in are on equal footing with all other activities, then why do we sense so strongly a chasm between them? Are we really to think that taking a nap is of equal weight in glory as praying? It seems perfectly sensible that there are some activities that glorify God more than others. Where then, are we going wrong?

To better understand how we glorify God, let us first understand the nature of God's glory. The biggest misconception of God's glory is in thinking that we can add to or increase God's glory. We can mistakenly believe that because we are able to glorify God, means that God's glory is quantitatively or qualitatively tied to us. This is a dreadful misunderstanding. God's glory cannot be diminished nor can it be added to, for the glory of God is in God being God and that finds full expression in the Trinity. If the glory of God was tied to us, Christ could not have said as he did, "glorify me in your presence with the glory I had with you before the world began" (John 17:5). God is perfectly sufficient within himself; God lacks nothing, including glory.

If we cannot increase God's glory, what then does it mean to glorify God? It means simply to reflect him. By reflecting God we testify and proclaim who God is, his character and his nature. But that does not mean we are *adding* to the glory of God for that would be like thinking a million dollars next to a mirror is worth two million.

I should perhaps alter the analogy just slightly to account for the phenomenon of perceived increase of God's glory on earth. A biblical analogy springs to mind. Let us think of God as the sun and we as mirrors reflecting his light. The perception of the sunbeams can be increased or diminished by the conditions of the mirrors. A clean mirror would give off more light than a dirty one, and a concentration of mirrors would be brighter and give off more heat than mirrors in isolation. In this way, the power and majesty of the sun's rays may be intensified and our perception and experience of it increased. But whether there are many mirrors or no mirrors, whether clean mirrors or covered mirrors, the sun itself is utterly uninfluenced, its brightness remains unaffected, its temperature unaltered, its intensity unchanged. It is the same with God and his glory. We may experience a greater manifestation of God's glory based on how we reflect him, but it is only a manifestation, for the glory of God remains unaltered. The glory of God may be more or less palpable, but never does it increase or diminish in grandeur.

Since we do not add to God's glory, but merely reflect it, we may begin to see how even our rudimentary carnal activities glorify God. All creation is a reflection of the creator; if we as creatures operate in accordance to our design, our designer is glorified. We are creatures that eat, and creatures that sleep, and creatures that play, and creatures that create, and creatures that enjoy stories, and jokes, and puzzles, and hobbies of all kinds. That is how we are made, and when we do the things that we were made to do, we reflect our maker, and that is God's glory.

Of course even though the carnal activities of homo sapiens glorifies God as creator, a distinction can still be made between our spiritual and physical selves, and therefore it could still be argued that our spiritual selves are superior in reflecting God. Since we know that God is spirit it cannot be our physical selves that were created in the image of God, and hence, our spiritual acts like prayer are superior to our physical acts, like sleep, in reflecting and glorifying God. By this reasoning we may still say that certain activities glorify God more, in the sense that they more accurately reflect him.

I think this argument makes an error in its representation of the *imago Dei*.[1] We were created whole with mind and body, and we are only ever whole with physical and spiritual together. The software and hardware together make the computer. I submit that the image of God does not reside in the physical or spiritual, but in the particular fusion of both. The duality and yet unity of our being is perhaps reflective of the triune nature of God. The *imago Dei* may be the synthesis of our components as one being, and perhaps finds full expression when we are no longer dual, but are mind, body, and Holy Spirit.

I think it is far more likely that the most accurate reflection of God that man can produce is not created by isolating man's components, but is expressed through the whole unified nature of man. As such, our so-called spiritual acts are not superior reflections of God but are important and necessary elements for reflecting God accurately. Still, more attention is certainly given to these activities than others, and that is for good reason.

If we were to whittle down every action we do that reflects God, we would find under them all a call to obedience. Obedience is at the heart of reflecting God, for any disobedience to God is by definition outside of God's will, and therefore at odds with his character and nature, which is God's glory. What is not of God does not reflect God, and you cannot glorify God with what is not godly.

Every command God has given us has its origin in the nature and character of God. Therefore, when we obey God's commands and precepts we reflect God's nature and character, which is his glory. The reason then, that there is such one-sided consideration given to the so-called spiritual actions over the unspiritual actions in glorifying God, is because a good deal of the unspiritual actions are compulsory, and so we see no disobedience. For example, God made us creatures that sleep; God designed us that way, for that was how he desired us to be. Now there is nobody who is rebelling against sleep, for sleep is compulsory. Every one of us sleeps, and in that way, we all comply with the desire and design of God.

---

1. *Imago Dei* is the concept of being created in the image of God.

The categorization of spiritual and unspiritual actions is really a farce, but the fact that we think in those terms is instructive. We tend to think that sleep is unspiritual, until sleep gives way to sloth. We tend to think that eating is unspiritual, until eating gives way to gluttony. It is compulsory for a man to eat and for a man to sleep, but is not compulsory for a man to be slothful or gluttonous. So what is compulsory is not regarded as being spiritual, and because it is compulsory there is no means for disobedience. God made us as creatures that sleep, and we fully comply with sleep, but God also made us creatures that are designed to worship him, and here we find a good deal of rebellion. This demonstrates that there are ways in which we reflect God that are compulsory, that are intrinsic, reflections as created beings, and that there are ways to reflect God through our free will. More attention is given to those reflections of God that are not only desired, (a man may desire or love sleep even if it is compulsory for man) but are willed, and deservedly so.

We have see then, that the reason we are more attentive to glorifying God through prayer, and fasting, and living pure lives is because such things come to us less naturally. Such means to reflect God are not compulsory, and they are not so readily desired. But that does not mean that the path to superior glorification of God is to strip away all those reflections of God that are natural and that come easy to us and replace them with what is difficult. Rather, everything we do that reflects God should continue, whether it be compulsory like our sleeping, or readily pleasing like enjoying the use of our talents, or profoundly difficult like loving our enemies.

Since God is glorified by our obedience, we should not think that we can better our reflection of God by a mere increase in perceived holy actions. The Scripture says, "Does the LORD delight in burnt offerings and sacrifices as much as in obeying the voice of the LORD? To obey is better than sacrifice, and to heed is better than the fat of rams" (1 Sam 15:20). The pertinent question then is not "how much are you reading your Bible," or "how many times a day do you pray" but rather, "are you obeying God?" There is no holy action, no devotional, no ministry, no church event, no sacrificial act that can glorify God without obedience.

I am not trying to cast aspersions on religious activities, as is the vogue, for religious activities are generally done out of obedience to God's decrees. I merely wish to demonstrate that an arbitrary increase in so-called spiritual actions does not equate to an increase of the glorification of God. The issue is of obedience, and notice that obedience is not a matter of degree. Either you are obeying God or you are disobeying him. The sensible thing to say if we want to glorify God *more* is that we need to cease in our lives the practice of that which disobeys God's commands and decrees. The insensible thing to say is that if we wish to glorify God more we must increase the amount of the practice that is *already* obedient to God. If a man faced ten stop signs on his route to work, and his co-worker only had five stop signs on his route, we would be foolish to think that the first man was somehow *more* obedient to the laws of traffic because he stopped at *ten* signs while the other man only stopped at *five*. In the same way, it is foolish to think that increasing the number of, let's say, prayers in your day will make you glorify God more if you are *already* being obedient to God in your prayer life.

I have attempted to make the case that our perceived unspiritual acts are not inglorious to God, and that God's glory is not increased by an increase in our spiritual acts. But I have in some sense been arguing against a straw man, for if we are honest, the problem we have in glorifying God is not in our misguided zealousness for spirituality, but in our overwhelming apathy for God. Who among us is really cutting back their hours of sleep just to have more time in prayer to God? I made the case that such an action is not necessary for those who are already obedient in prayer, but we are *not* obedient. The reality is there are many Christians who day in and day out do not speak to their Savior. They do not heed the word of God to, "be joyful always; *pray continually*, give thanks in all circumstances, for this is God's *will* for you in Christ Jesus" (1 Thess 5:16–18; emphasis mine). There is no condemnation for watching television, or surfing the web, or enjoying a hobby, but there is much to condemn for those who do those things but are not in the word of God. We ought to devote ourselves to the reading of Scripture, and heed its advice. "Do not let this Book of the Law depart from your mouth, meditate on it day and night, so that you may be careful to do everything written in it" (Josh 1:8). Also, "devote yourself to the public reading of Scripture, to preaching and to teaching" (1 Tim 4:13). This is good advice given to Joshua and Timothy, and it is good advice for us as well. We know that it is good for us to read the Bible regularly, and we know that anyone, then, who knows the good he ought to do and does not do it, sins (Jas 4:17).

Now we are not being inglorious to God simply because we watch a television show or take a nap, or undertake any other commonly classified unspiritual activity. We have freedom in Christ, though we must be obedient to him. Indeed, the passage of Scripture most often cited when discussing glorifying God is in actuality examining the believer's freedom. The Apostle Paul says, "'Everything is permissible'—but not everything is constructive. Nobody should seek his own good, but the good of others" (1 Cor 10:23-24). From this as a basis, Paul demonstrates that eating meat sacrificed to idols is not inherently immoral or inglorious to God, but if our free act is done at the expense of another man's conscience it becomes iniquitous. The Apostle Paul concludes his discussion on eating sacrificed meat by stating, "So whether you eat or drink or whatever you do, do it all for the glory of God. Do not cause anyone to stumble, whether Jews, Greeks or the church of God—even as I try to please everybody in every way" (1 Cor 10:31-33). In view of the context it becomes clearer what the Apostle Paul means by glorifying God in all ways. It is precisely what we stated: obey God in everything you do. There is nothing disobedient about eating food sacrificed to idols, but if it causes your brother to stumble, you are then being disobedient to the command to love your brother, and to be charitable.

For the same reason we are free to engage in all kinds of activities so long as we continue to be obedient to God. Now the great difficultly in having such freedom is that it becomes more exacting to discern what it is that we ought to do in order to glorify God. There are times when even a sound principle, like "do not cause your brother to stumble," must be neglected in order to be obedient to God. There are moments when doing what is right, when doing what God has called you to do, will cause your brother to sin by means of envy, or anger, or spiritual confusion. At all times, but particularly in these cases we must be vigilant to check our motives and actions, to hold them up to the light of Scripture and the moving of the Holy Spirit to test if they are holy or not. It is a real trick for the devil to incite you to harm your brother, but it is a more pleasing trick to our enemy, if you would harm your brother while thinking you are the more righteous for doing so.

The sad and regrettable reality is that much of the abuse of the believer's freedom is not even cleverly cloaked in phony righteous ministry, but is found in the most trivial of things. We find it in the consumption of alcohol, in the occasional smoke, in the brandishing of piercings and tattoos, in the clothing we wear, especially of women, and in the movies, music, and books that we partake of. All of these things are mere trivialities and yet at some point or another we are all perhaps guilty of desiring these ahead of the good of another, and at the expense of the conscience of our brothers and sisters. Such actions do not glorify God.

Protests have probably come to mind with great rapidity. "But there *is* nothing wrong with having a beer, or a glass of wine," you might plead. Or, "What is wrong with having a nose ring, or a tattoo?" "Do I have to wear a burka or throw my make-up in the trash, just to be sure no one is stumbling?" "Must I burn my Harry Potter books because some are offended by the depiction of magic in fiction?" The whole scenario strikes us as being terribly unfair. It feels as though our freedom is being stripped from us by the ignorance of another.

I am deeply sympathetic to these protests. Much of the squawking on issues of propriety seems to originate in those who are the most ill informed. Indeed, the loss of our freedom is due to the deficiency of another. We cannot drink because some cannot handle a drink. We cannot wear what is culturally fashionable because some have lustful eyes. We cannot openly enjoy a book, or a song, or a movie, because some are lacking in hermeneutical skills. We cannot have our freedom because some are ignorant of the freedom that is in Christ. The very problem that we have with this is, that it is so antithetical to our nature that those we deem *wrong* should get their way.

It seems so unfair that ignorance should be accommodated and that the biggest prude should get his way. Would it not be better to sit down and correct the backward thinking, rather than conceding our freedoms to accommodate them? If only we could say once and for all, that there is nothing wrong with eating food sacrificed to idols. Would it not be better to simply explain that the appropriateness of dress is relative to the culture, and therefore to be in fashion is not necessarily to be immodest? Or to explain, that a note is not more holy simply because it is played by a Christian band, or that a movie is not more godly because it is free from swear words.

I think that there is a place for correction, after all, the Apostle Paul, even in telling us to be accommodating and to think of others, makes his case for why eating food sacrificed to idols is not in fact immoral (1 Cor 10:25–30). In need of most correction, in my view, is the modern Christian's hermeneutical skills. It is quite distressing to me that there are those who are appalled at profanity in films and yet see nothing wrong with something like *The Wizard of Oz*, which is a film that can easily be construed to espouse that God, as symbolically portrayed in the wizard, does not exist, and that salvation comes from within. Nothing could be more profane, and yet simply because no curses stem from the lips of Dorothy and crew it is regarded as a morally sanitary film. The lack of hermeneutical consideration needs to be examined, and there is a place for correction, and a loving manner in which to correct.

However, in manners of such trivial things, correction has the tendency to instigate petty quarrels. This, we are explicitly warned against in Scripture. "Don't have anything to do with foolish and stupid arguments, because you know they produce quarrels. And the Lord's servant must not quarrel; instead, he must be kind to everyone, able to teach, not resentful" (2 Tim 2:23–24). Correction is good, but silence might be better. Refraining from conflict is preferable in lieu of the common form our correction takes. Typically, to correct bad thinking we antagonize. Disturbingly, we will not alter our behavior to accommodate our fellow brother, but we will do so to goad them. We will be more excessive with our freedoms just to prove that we have the freedom. We will flaunt our tastes in wine, we will dress more provocatively, and we will further the display of our body art until at last we have prodded them enough so that they come and speak to us. Then we will, oh so very gently, correct them and explain how wrong and stupid they are. When we only see the exercise of our freedoms as someone else's problem, then it is we who have a problem.

We have freedom, but we must glorify God. We have freedom, but let us never disobey God's commands and decrees. So long as you are fully obedient to God, you may dress as you like and glorify him. So long as you are fully obedient to God, you may have your wine and your beer and glorify God. So long as you are fully obedient to God you may have your books, and your video games, and your movies and glorify God.

On the subject of the entertainment arts there may be much disagreement. If it is demonstrable that watching the movies you watch or listening to the music you listen to is disobedient to God's calling to live pure lives, then obviously we cannot partake of that and glorify God. Entire subculture industries have been formed believing that the consumption of morally questionable secular entertainment is inglorious to God. In light of that, their mission is to present a supposedly safe alternative to the secular offerings. In support of that position the passage most often quoted is Philippians 4:8 which declares, "Finally, brothers, whatever is true, whatever is noble, whatever is right, whatever is pure, whatever is lovely, whatever is admirable—if anything is excellent or praiseworthy—think about such things."

There is no question that we as Christians are called to purity. The Scripture says, "Set your minds on things above, not on earthly things" (Col 3:2). It says to, "Flee the evil desires of youth, and pursue righteousness, faith, love and peace, along with those who call on the Lord out of a pure heart" (2 Tim 2:22). It is very well established that we should be pure: pure in our thoughts, and in our actions. However, if we are going to appropriately address the impurity of consuming certain content, we must firmly establish what it is that makes it impure.

Let us first dispense with the very silly notion that the mere act of seeing, or hearing, or processing messages that are contrary to God is the act of impurity. If that were the case we could not converse with a nonbeliever for fear that they would speak, and we would hear a message that is contrary to God and thereby be impure. To seclude one's self, to plug one's eyes and ears as a means to purity is to mistake ignorance for innocence. Though few would be foolish enough to explicitly state that they believe innocence *is* ignorance, there are many who live as though it were, as if the mere act of watching a television show with ungodly actions is itself impure. But ignorance cannot be innocence, for the very simple reason that God, who is perfectly holy, perfectly pure, is also all knowing.

The omniscient mind cannot be ignorant. God has seen and heard all messages that are contrary to him. God has seen every impure thought, every horrific deed, every evil action, and he knows completely every ungodly theme in every film, or book, or lyric of music. God's exposure to it does not make him impure, for God is not corrupted by it. The Bible says, "To the pure, all things are pure, but to those who are corrupted and do not believe, nothing is pure. In fact, both their minds and their consciences are corrupted" (Titus 1:15). Jesus said, "First clean the inside of the cup and dish, and then the outside also will be clean" (Matt 23:26). The impurity of ourselves comes from within, not from without. We stand aghast and deride those "dirty rotten shows" when instead we ought to deride our dirty rotten selves. Perversion sells only because the world is full of perverts.

We must remember that to the pure all things are pure, and that everything is permissible, but not everything is constructive. It is not impure or disobedient for us to watch *The Wizard of Oz*, even though, as we have discussed, it thematically champions humanism, an unwise and ungodly philosophy; so long as the ungodly elements of the film do not lead us to disobedience, we are free to enjoy the merry songs and colorful characters and still regard the theme correctly as a loathsome lie. As long as we continue to see the good *as* good and evil *as* evil we may see all things and not be impure. Mere exposure to impurity does not make you impure. The entertainment arts do not *cause* sin, but they do entice it.

We are all tempted by various things, and the messages and content of media may serve as our eager tempters. But what powerfully tempts one man may be of no real temptation to another. *The Wizard of Oz* is for me innocuous, because the philosophy of humanism has never been a big temptation for me, but that may not be said for everyone. Likewise, there may be much that others may partake of without danger of falling to disobedience, but which, might likely ensnare me. We should not think ourselves better than we are, or be tricked by naïveté. We know what tempts us, and we must guard our hearts and our minds, and flee from our tempters. But to be tempted is not to sin; therefore, you are free to consume whatever media you would like so long as you do not disobey the commands and decrees of God. In your freedom be careful, so that you may glorify God in everything you do.

We must strive in every way we can to glorify God, not by special actions deemed more spiritual, but by full obedience to God's will, and commands, and decrees for our lives. There is no action by which we may increase or diminish the glory of God, but we may affect the manifestation of his glory around us by our obedience. In all of our daily activities, in all of our spiritual deeds, in all of our banal actions, in all of our freedoms, let us be found to be obedient to God, and thereby glorify him.

Conclusion

WE HAVE COME TO the end of our examination of the fine print of Christianity. Though by no means exhaustive, I have addressed what I feel are the truisms of Christianity that are most readily expressed. We have inspected the axioms associated with the nature of God, as well as the platitudes espoused about the Christian life, and although you may disagree with some of my answers, I hope we can all agree that pat answers will no longer do. If nothing else, let us proclaim that the theology of Christianity is too rich and complex to fit on a bumper sticker, and that the quick answer is an insufficient one.

I would consider it a victory if this book serves as a good caution against hyping the tenets of Christianity, or marketing the promises of God. Truth is not a sales pitch, and for too long the church has sought to satisfy its constituents rather than enlighten. We have propagated the bold print and consequently have spread a superficial understanding of our faith, which is a faith destined to fail, a faith that will not stand up to tough scrutiny or correspond with reality. This book, I hope, is one step in correcting that. There is a deeper truth in Christianity than the truisms that are told, let us not settle for the superficial, or be content with hollow clichés, but rather, let us fully embrace the difficult, the baffling, the seemingly dissatisfying, and yet perfectly, beautifully, real Christianity.

Bibliography

Associated Press. "Power of Prayer Flunks An Unusual Test." No pages. Online: http://www.msnbc.msn.com/id/12082681/.

Craig, William Lane. *Time And Eternity: Exploring God's Relationship To Time*. Wheaton: Crossway, 2001.

Grudem, Wayne. *Systematic Theology*. Grand Rapids: Zondervan, 2000.

Haldane, J. B. S. *Possible worlds and other essays*. London: Chattto & Windus, 1927.

Lewis, C. S. *Mere Christianity*. New York: Harper Collins, 2001.

———. *The Problem of Pain*. New York: Harper Collins, 2001. First published 1944 by Macmillan.

Williams, Debra. "Can the Power of Prayer be Proven?" No pages. Online: http://www.plim.org/PrayerDeb.htm.

www.ingramcontent.com/pod-product-compliance
Lightning Source LLC
Chambersburg PA
CBHW070943160426
43193CB00011B/1797